I05O3684

INVEST IN
REAL ESTATE

(How to Create Wealth and Passive Income
With a Smart Guide for Beginners)

BY

James H. Johnson

© Copyright 2019 by James H. Johnson

Disclaimer

◆ ◆ ◆

All erudition contained in this book is given for informational and educational purposes only. The author is not in any way accountable for any results or outcomes that emanate from using this material. Constructive attempts have been made to provide information that is both accurate and effective, but the author is not bound for the accuracy or use/misuse of this information.

Foreword

I would like to thank you for taking the first step of trusting me and deciding to purchase/read this life-transforming eBook. Thanks for spending your time and resources on this material.

I can assure you of exact results if you will diligently follow this blueprint, I lay bare in the information manual you are currently reading. It has transformed lives, and I strongly believe it will equally transform yours too.

All the information I presented in this Do It Yourself piece is easy to digest and practice.

TABLE OF CONTENTS

Introduction 7

Chapter One The Meaning Of Real Estate............................... 20

Chapter Two A Solid Plan For Getting Started, Even With Limited Capital 46

Chapter Three Important Things To Note While Embarking On A Real Estate Business 63

Chapter Four Finding The Best Market/Price For Your Investment Portfolio Should Be For Your Budget.................. 79

Chapter Five How To Profit From Real Estate Without Owning Any Property 102

Chapter Six How To Determine A Good Rental Property 116

Chapter Seven How To Determine What Type Of Rental To Buy.. 135

Chapter Eight How To Find Low Cost Properties 150

Chapter Nine How To Set The Right Price For Your Real Estate Listing.. 166

Chapter Ten How To Finance Rentals 182

INTRODUCTION

◆ ◆ ◆

In this book, we're divulging Real Estate Adventures – an improvement of real estate Experiences that incorporates the mind boggling open door for interesting visitors to channel their inner Phileas Fogg and tour around the world in eighty days. This epic voyage over six of the Earth's landmasses joins exceptional adventures now on hand to book through hosts on real estate, extending from following lions via strolling with Sabache Warriors in Kenya to chasing UFOs with Nate in Arizona.

The climb in the number of property holders who are overburdened by their mortgages has expanded so much that a remarkably large number of them have inferred that they can't continue to keep on being in their homes. They would chose to sell and buy a similar residential at a much lower cost. They would improve their living conditions and life in general by having a lower mortgage portion every single month. Considering there is no shortage of properties to buy, these people would have no trouble finding a functional home at an OK cost.

Likewise, some other delayed consequence of the increase in open houses is that many of those people who are in the market are first-time property holders. Since costs on homes are falling, a consistently growing number of people can control the expense of a household for a comparable total they are at present paying in rent. So the shrewd decision for these people is to buy a house instead of renting.

These factors all lead to real estate agents having to support the buying and promoting of these properties. Regardless of the fact that prices have fallen, the number of properties, purchasers, and sellers has risen making the market quite competitive. This is the kind of market that many real estate agents like to operate in. It's profitable for them as properties are available and so are buyers.

The difficulty comes in when a real estate professional has exhausted their current client list. The best route for them to get more customers is through one way or another, get extra real estate leads. In addition to the reality that they need extra leads, they need great leads; high quality leads that will convert to a client who will genuinely close on purchasing or selling at least one property.

So how might you get greater real estate leads? There are obviously a wide range of ways. These include getting them from a company that offers them, promoting, shopping for them on lead sites, developing and maintaining your personal real estate website that draws possible customers to it, and through getting them via your personal system. There are other techniques for creating real estate leads too, but these are the most extensively used strategies - all of which have proven to work in a specific way.

Perhaps the most ordinary strategies to get real estate leads are with the aid of buying them. Sellers provide this information to people who are eager to pay for it. So in the event that you are a real estate professional searching for leads and unable to find your own, this might be a first option for you.

You have to then filter through them and make sense of the information yourself. You will then need to see if these leads are reliable or not.

Obtaining real estate leads or shopping for them can be costly. This can be a terrible element considering the fact that the whole goal of buying leads is to find customers, promote properties, and make commissions, if the leads that you purchase do not seriously turn into commissions. All things considered, not only did you not sell any property (or several properties), but you squandered money on useless data, and you sat around idly ending up with useless leads.

Another strategy to produce real estate leads is with through advertising. If you are a real estate operator, dealer, or agent, advertising your services might be the best method to produce real estate leads. This kind of lead will help you discover people who want to buy or sell property; the tables are turned and they come searching for you.

Added to this, there is another advantage to advertising. The people who are trying to find you are truthfully eager to purchase or sell property. This means that you do not have to stress over whether or not they are going to end up being good leads, they most likely will be.

Another technique to produce real estate leads is to create your own website. Sites are economical to build and maintain, and having one created for you does not need to be costly either. What's more, if you have the skills to build one yourself this is an added bonus. You are able to keep the site as up to date as you please which might be difficult if someone else does it.

The motivations to keep your website current cannot be downplayed. To start with, you want to refresh with new homes continuously so the persons who visit your web page will always have something to look at. Considering this list of properties will change many times as your consumer list develops and transforms, you will have to update your website frequently with the new residences and remove the ones that are no longer available.

A second rationalization in the back of keeping your website up to date all the time is that your page rank will be higher. Web indexes utilize a number of factors to decide that they are so relevant to specific terms, and the place to show them in a list of question items. So the added benefit to updating your site is that it increases the chance to rank your page high. This means that it's going to show up when a user inputs questions that match with real estate terms and phrases, and the guests will get to know of and visit your site.

When you get visitors to your site, you may be getting the opportunity you need to convert them into clients. They can stay on your website online for some length of time to take a look at as few or as many houses as they want to. Your website makes it possible for many to look at one property simultaneously, that is something that you probably would not be able to do face to face. This is what is regarded as impact, and the effect is that you can radically change a personal mission into a fortune 500 business.

Another option to garner leads is to host events. It enables you to build up clientele thereby providing you with a pool of people who are either interested in buying or selling property. This is probably one of the best techniques that you can use but it is also one of the most difficult.

The first thing you'll have to do is to start building your system. You won't need a whole lot to start. Keeping your ear on the ground and networking is important in this strategy. It helps you build up a list of people who will be important to make the system work. These people will be useful in spreading the word about your business both face-to-face and online.

With all these options of creating lead, a very simple way to do it is in your daily life. You can tell people about what you do for work at the market, library, church, in line at the bank, or anywhere. The more dedicated you are to it, the quicker you will have the chance to advance your system and the happier you will be in the long run. People will start spreading the word and your clientele can grow easily. Word of mouth is very useful in this type of business.

Always have business cards with your contact details when you're organizing events or networking to get more clients. That way you do not simply rely on individual's memory which is not the most reliable.

Cards also present a professional image which can direct clients your way.

If you are searching for rental property as investment, then so much caution must be taken. Before you set out on your journey for a rental property, ensure that you really understand what it resembles to be a landowner. In spite of the fact that it is a profitable endeavor, it's anything but easy owning or managing these properties. You would need to keep up the property so as to receive the monetary benefits all through the time of your ownership.

To many, rental property investment is basically something that includes purchasing a house, giving it on lease, and after that rounding up bucks while unwinding in a sofa. This is a long way from being realistic, especially if you wish for a regular rental income for a considerable length of time to come. Owning a rental property and accumulating a sound rental salary for a year or two is only a commonplace undertaking. However, keeping up a long lasting rental income until you sell the property is the thing that requires more effort on your part.

Being an investor, there is nothing more awful than keeping an empty rental property. This is because you would need to use up your own assets for the upkeep of the property which isn't giving you any profits when it's empty. Consequently, you ought to effectively look for tenants and do whatever is conceivable to keep them in the property. This includes paying attention to the requirements of the tenants and making repairs when necessary. You may do some minor repairs without anyone else's input, however, other complex repairs (fixing drainage and windowpanes) are best left to a specialist.

As you continue to look for rental property investment, it is essential that you think about the area. This involves considering the separation of the property from your living arrangement, the accessibility of tenants, the normal lease that you can earn, and the capacity of occupants in the region to pay you. A few areas may demonstrate more worth investing in than others. For example, it is smarter to lease a house close by a school, since a dreadful number of people are probably going to look for a home in the region of their school. This results in a lot of options for occupants throughout the entire year. In a nutshell, rental property investment is tied in with investigating the area, taking the necessary steps to lease your property, keeping your tenants happy, and keeping up the property so it remains occupied for quite a long time.

Investment in rental property can be a dangerous choice if the investor has not done his/her study well. For the investor who has set aside the effort to look into everything, it tends to be rewarding. The one thing most investors need to know more than everything else is the means by which they can wind up wealthy in the quickest timeframe putting resources into rental property.

Most investors are caught up with focusing on flipping single-family houses, when they ought to focus on putting resources into multi-occupancies. With a single family house, on the off chance that you lose the leaseholder, you have lost 100% of your salary which could be your profits for a whole year. However, if you have a four-family condo and lose a tenant, you have three different families giving you checks to cover your costs. The primary concern is income and income is more assured with multi-occupancy properties than with single-occupancy families.

In the event that you have put resources into a few single-family rental properties you will more than likely need to make a trip to a few different areas to collect funds, or to mind the property. With one multi-occupancy property you spare time, gas and mileage on your vehicle by just going to one area to collect your funds, or to keep an eye on your property. With the present economy, it could cost from $2000-$7500 relying upon where in the country it is and the size of the house. Increase that by six and you're talking an extremely huge income of cash. Fixing a six-family roof would cost between $5000-$10,000. You can figure it out.

There are a great deal of real estate masters with infomercials talking about the cash to be made from flipping houses. They let it to appear to be simple. You will before long realize that it tends to be difficult flipping a house, particularly if you don't check the house out properly a long time before purchasing. Costly, yet very tedious. Also the various temporary workers you need to manage. That is another issue; setting aside the effort to meeting and researching every one of those temporary workers. All things considered, you need somebody who knows what they are doing, isn't that right? When you locate a decent temporary worker and he has done work for you, don't think that they will always be prepared to hop when you call them. They are specialists and they can't lounge around waiting for your calls. They have different irons in the flame like all great representatives.

Try not to misunderstand me, investment in rental property is a decent business. Single-family houses are wise investments. Yet, there is the option to invest your resources into multi-occupancies. If you are aware of any individual who is making cash flipping houses, chances are that the person also has a few rentals in their portfolio. Flipping houses is fine for the individual who needs to do it, however, investment in rental property is the better investment. Furthermore, there is a huge market for investing in multi-occupancies.

The primary rental property classes comprise of single-family rental properties, multi-occupancy private rental properties, business rental properties and holiday homes. Here are different focuses to consider with rental property investments:

1) Repossessions, fixer-uppers, and probate homes are good options for property investment. Rentals can be very valuable which helps you to achieve positive income from leasing. Purchasing fixer upper homes or repossessions can lessen cash used for investment and can therefore improve on the income to get from renting them out.

2) One can't expect an impressive income from property with one tenant. For this situation, the only objective is to cover the home loan and current costs.

3) Research on a potential rental home should incorporate critical money related plans and arrangements for years ahead, similar to costs of property management, renovations and repairs, crisis and so on.

4) The 2-4 unit homes are the best options for multi-unit private property investments.

5) With condo investments the fundamental benefit originates from the rental income. A rent to buy alternative and utilizing investment cash is very helpful

for this situation. The most noteworthy factors for this situation are the money related assessment and property management. With a steady income from various occupants, it is best to have a director for the property management.

6) Commercial properties investments incorporate places of business, retail malls, mechanical properties and so forth. The market estimation of these properties is settled on the income (net rental pay). The fundamental goal of rental in these cases is to create enough money to surpass the expense of home loan, protection, upkeep, future enhancements. This isn't a simple business to deal with. It requires investigation of numerous things. Yet, whenever done appropriately it could prove to be worthwhile. Changes in the financial conditions typically affect these sorts of real estate investments more than private property investments. Furthermore, commercial properties are progressively vulnerable to these changes, it is smart to keep additional money aside to help those investments if something does not go true to form. For this situation, a cash utilizing approach (rent to buy alternative) is helpful.

7) A holiday home can be utilized in two different ways. It tends to be a second home or an investment property. This classification incorporates resort properties, country homes, or beach homes. With holiday rentals, the benefit originates from the appreciation. Income

produced from leasing is typically utilized for costs like property management, home loan and protection. These are transient rentals and require a lot of upkeep.

CHAPTER ONE
THE MEANING OF REAL ESTATE

◆ ◆ ◆

A quick search on Google will probably get you an enormous scope of results. On the off chance that you find a property on a real estate website, you can typically look at photographs on the web and potentially take a virtual visit. You would then be able to test distinctive web goals, for instance, assess the neighborhood, get an idea of the property's estimation, see what the current owner paid for it, look at the monthly charges, get enlistment data, school information, and even see what retail outlets are in the neighborhood by virtually walking around, all without going out!

The Business of Real Estate

Land is typically bought and offered either through an approved real estate administrator or the owner. Most are acquired and offered through real estate delegates.

(We use "administrator" and "master" to imply a real estate personnel.) This is because of the reality of their real estate picking up information of and trip and, at any rate for the most part, their pick get passage to a database of dynamic houses open to be acquired. This is to access to this database of property postings gave the finest methodology to examine for properties.

A great part of the time, available to be bought by-owner houses cannot be honestly brought to a MLS and CIE, which are as a rule set aside by methods for REALTOR affiliations. The nonattendance of a supervised centered database can make these homes relentlessly hard to discover. Generally, these homes are found through looking round or scanning advertisements in the local paper's real estate postings. A progressively fabulous strategy to arrange available to be obtained by-owner houses is to show up for an open to be bought by-owner website in the geographic zone.

Who is a REALTOR? To a great extent the terms real estate administrator and REALTOR are used interchangeably. A REALTOR is an approved real estate administrator who is in like manner a male or female from the NATIONAL ASSOCIATION OF REALTORS. They are required to consent to a demanding code of ethics and lead.

MLS and CIE property presenting records utilized on be for all intents and purposes only reachable in printed form, and as we referenced, just genuinely open to real estate administrators people from a MLS or CIE. Around ten years back, this essential property information began to move out to the internet.

One legitimization is that most of the 1 million or so REALTORS have websites, and the far-reaching larger part of those websites have fluctuating proportions of the near to MLS or CIE property insights affirmed on them. Another defense is that there are various non-real estate master websites that similarly give real estate information, including, close by to be acquired by-owner regions, dispossession districts, regional and worldwide postings, County assessor regions, and valuation and market actualities regions.

Realtors

Notwithstanding, the flood of real estate information on the internet, most homes are so far sold truly through real estate administrators posting properties in the territorial MLS or CIE. Regardless, these property postings don't remain on the market any more. By its inclination, the internet is a worldwide business focus and neighborhood MLS and CIE postings are regularly unfurled for show on a colossal scope of Web goals. For example, many go to the NATIONAL ASSOCIATION OF REALTORS website, http://www.realtor.com, and to the near to real estate administrator's website page. Additionally, the posting would perhaps be demonstrated on the website page of a near to paper.

Despite internet advertising, posting administrators may moreover enable the trader to decide on a price, keep open houses, sort out the settlement and help with closing. When an expert offers these services it is insinuated equivalent to a full help posting way of activity.

Changes in the advancement at the back of the real estate business have made various administrators change the way they work. In large part, this is a result of the second get to most customers as of now need to property postings and other real estate information. Likewise, the internet and unmistakable headways have robotized an extraordinary period of the publicizing and advertising and initial filtering process for real estate. For example, customers can see houses on the net and make solicits with the guide from limit of email. Agents can utilize automated activities to deliver postings to purchasers that fits their property criteria. Along these lines, administrators limit the services they offer and may change their costs in like manner. An administrator may offer to advance the property in the MLS yet simply give constrained more noteworthy organizations. Later on, some real estate administrators can likewise offer organizations in a higher measure of an ala carte style.

Due to the volume of real estate statistics on the internet, when men and women enlist a real estate expert they have to take a look at the unique services provided based on their needs. Purchasers and sellers alike depend on referrals. The internet presently makes it possible to discover certified realtors and to these how a professional is in the industry through reviews and customer feedback. One such site, AgentWorld.com, which is quickly turning into the LinkedIn or Facebook for real estate specialists. On this website an expert can customize their profile, start a blog, submit snap shots and recordings and even link their accounts to their sites.

Some have contended that the internet makes REALTORS and the MLS less significant. This is something I disagree with personally. Being available on the internet allows learned, qualified, and trained REALTORS more better access to the market and vice versa. Surely, the quantity of real estate professionals has risen altogether lately. The internet is merely a way for all these realtors to do their job better. Acquiring/purchasing property is probably the biggest single purchase decision that most will make in their life and they want professional help. Being available online allows for that help to be more accessible.

Online real estate is an awesome avenue for consumers and sellers alike and a promoting machine for realtors. When utilized appropriately, buyers can save time by quickly looking at houses and, eventually settle on what they want to buy. Sellers can productively inquire about the market and settle on enlisting the services of a specialist and advertising their properties on the internet through them. The next stage is to understand where to look online for the best properties.

Web Strategies

In the segments that follow, we provide techniques and guidelines on how to make use of the internet to find residences available for purchase and how to look into the statistics applicable to your preferences. There are several real estate websites from which to choose., One strategy to test a website's exactness is to scan for statistics about a property you have information on; this could be a property you own or one friends or families own.

Discovering real estate available for sale

MLS databases present a wide variety of real estate data. Most now provide different web destinations (principally managed by real estate specialists). A good example is the NAR webpage, realtor.com, which is the most outstanding website for looking real estate postings. Realtor.com exhibits quite a few dynamic posting stock of available properties.

To get all the information you will need to find a licensed close by realtor. Numerous nearby real estate operators will likewise supply their consumers (by email) new postings that are available on the MLS with their predefined criteria. This can be useful to a purchaser who is actively looking for property.

There are additionally many local sites that show real estate experts in the area along with their available properties. A large portion of great properties can be found on zillow.com and trulia.com. These sites provide specific administrations as well. For instance, zillow.com is known for its on-the-spot property valuation work and trulia.com for providing verifiable data. Another source of residences available to be purchased is the state, provincial, and close by websites related with financier organizations; for instance, remax.com or prudential.com. Web indexes like yahoo.com and grouped publicizing sites like craigslist.com have limitless dynamic real estate postings.

One key distinction between these sites is the statistics you can access namelessly. For instance, at trulia.com you can keep surf and view properties without an account up to the point that you have to navigate to the operator's webpage for more data. Numerous new real estate web indexes allow you to filter through postings 27based on your own criteria. The best technique is to try searching multiple sites. When you find a property that you like, locate a certified realtor of your choice to lead a whole pursuit in the nearby MLS.

Valuing Real Estate

As we referenced, one of the most well recognized real estate features of zillow.com is property valuation. Simply search in an area, find a property and get the property estimation. It even provides information about positive features of the area and negative points, and states the final date sold and the property charges. There are distinctive sites that supply same information, for example, housevalues.com and homegain.com. Tragically, numerous men and women make use of these evaluated traits alone to legitimize offers, costs, and counteroffers. These are sometimes just harsh assessments established on an equation that consolidates the district's data. These critiques can change dramatically over a quick timeframe and don't appear to persistently comply with real market changes, which are usually slow. Also, these appraisals don't naturally consider property redesigns or remodels or other property features or new changes. This is not to say these destinations are not valuable or the valuation is always wrong. Actually, they are magnificent starting points and can provide a first rate ball-park figure.

With regards to getting a precise value for a particular property, there are special methodologies that are progressively dependable. One is to go directly to your district's website. As a popular rule, the province assessor's vicinity's site offers and expense records of all houses in the district. If you want to investigate a specific property, this is useful source. When you go to a region's webpage you are getting records directly from the source. Most districts today distribute property data on their webpage. You cannot simply take a look at the price the previous landowner paid, but you can access the surveyed worth, property charges, and maps.

Given the significance of valuation, we are going to help you remember the two biggest (non-internet) valuation techniques: real estate operators and appraisers. Working with a nearby realtor is a specific method to get the right statistics for a property. While one of the major roles of the MLS is to showcase the dynamic property postings of its individuals, the framework additionally gathers statistics for these postings. Real estate professionals can pull this enterprise data and produce comparative market analysis (CMAs) that provide an amazing preview of a specific property's estimation for the market in a specific territory.

The most genuine method to estimate the price of a property is by using an assured appraiser to carry out an examination. An appraiser will oftentimes audit both the facts in the MLS framework along with the area records and after that create a valuation for the property established on at least one affirmed technique for valuation. These methods for valuation can incorporate an inspection of comparable properties for contrasts between the properties, figure out the cost to fix the property, and figure out its worth based on the income produced from the property.

The Neighborhood

There are several ways the internet can enable you to get the scoop on a specific neighborhood. For instance, enumeration records can be found at census.gov. You can likewise get information about the neighborhood on websites like outside.in or survey nearby on-line journals. A weblog is a website where individuals have a look at topics which have been discussed through messages. Start by taking a look at placeblogger.com and kcnn.org/citymediasites.com for a registry of sites. Trulia.com has a "Warmth Map" that suggests how warm or cold each and every place is depending on costs, deals, or prevalence among the local clients.

Schools

With regards to selling private property or funding residences that take into account families, the nature of the region school vicinity has an extensive effect. There are many websites which provide classification data.

Look at greatschools.net or schoolmatters.com. Most regional faculty areas likewise have their very own website. These sites include an assortment of data about country funded colleges and the faculty region, such as its socioeconomics, test scores, and mum or dad surveys.

Finding the Right Real Estate Agent

With the growth of the internet real estate information is available on websites that allow real estate operators to advertise their services by way of showing their expert profiles and socially connecting with web journals. You can find a realtor with unique skills, geographic territory of specialization, or an expert supplying explicit administrations. The website AgentWorld.com lets buyers quickly and effectively discover a professional with the right skills by making use of keyword searches. AgentWorld.com also allows experts to submit custom-made on line journals, pictures and recordings to allow buyers to choose the best operator for their needs. In addition, several operator profiles include a way to quickly connect to the specialist's website where you will likely be able to view their listings.

Maps and Other Tools

The internet has made mapping and discovering houses a lot simpler. To get an expanded or satellite view of a property or neighborhood, go to maps.live.com, maps.google.com or go to walkscore.com. These websites can give you an idea of the neighborhood qualities and the varieties of entertainment, cafés, and distinctive offices that are close to the property. Maps.Live.com offers a view that enables you to see the face of homes and Maps. Google even gives you a 360 degree view for specific neighborhoods. If you haven't tried these out yet, you should give them a try now.

Final Thoughts on Internet Strategies

The internet is a good lookup and advertising tool for real estate buyers, sellers and realtors alike. The internet can allow you to use less time and thereby make it faster to research properties. Websites like AgentWorld.com help you to productively find realtors who match your purchasing or selling needs.

Are there people in your town who don't see you as an expert in real estate? If this is true, it means that you are not showcasing your skills or business well and you could look into the strategies provided earlier in the chapter that can help you with this. I encounter real estate professionals all the time who aren't networking in their community and are therefore not getting the leads they require to do their job well. By advertising your services, hosting events and implementing any of the previously mentioned strategies, people will become aware of the services you offer and you will ultimately become a go-to realtor in your community.

Today, most property searches start on the internet. A quick keyword search on Google with the useful resource of location will get you a wide variety of results. If you find a property you like on a real estate site, you can then check all the information to see whether you will like the area. You can get registration information, university data, look at the real estate charges, neighborhood information, and even simply check retail shops!

Arranged Ads

The use of ads for getting information out about properties is probably one of the most useful tools for realtors and sellers. Although it can be expensive and there are occasions when it doesn't result in telephone calls or expressed interests, it is still important and useful. Spending about $350.00 a month for promotion is money well spent. I'd consider running ads 365 days per year to ensure that everyone in your area know that you are a realtor and you buy/sell real estate in their district.

Over the years, I have witnessed realtors and real estate companies advertising strategies that just does not work. Most run them for a set number of days or even only two or three weeks. Marketing real estate essentially doesn't work along these lines. Put your advertisement in the paper and leave it in there. You will more than make back the money you invested in advertising after the first sale. Don't be concerned with the fact that there are multiple other companies also advertising in your area. They are there on the grounds that they are getting reactions and they are in the business for the same reason you are – to make a living. Simply make certain to focus on your own real estate strategy and keep running your advertisement all the time else you'll be wasting your money.

When a new real estate ad appears in my paper, I will consistently check the ad. Almost nine times out of 10 I get through to a messaging system or an automatic email. This is a turn off for someone who is looking for property. They need to be able to reach someone when they call through to the number or email the address provided, they need to get a quick response. Get a number and an email address that you will be always have access to and be able to respond quickly. I myself have attempted different strategies and the one I have now has not changed for more than four years. I haven't changed it because I get the reactions that I need. My promotion is:

We Pay CASH FOR HOMES In 24 Hours! Any region, cost or condition Call xxx-xxx-xxxx

Find something that works for you and keep using it.

Promotions in the "Complimentary newspapers"

You may likewise run commercials in the complimentary newspapers in your community or the area you need to direct you real estate venture. These are the "Frugal Nickel," or whatever they are called in your area. This will usually cost you about $175.00 or so per month. They pull in opportunities quite well and have consistently justified the expenses. Keep in mind that people are typically open to negotiating on your rates.

Road Signs

Road signs are incredible! They are probably the best lead delivering tools around. I still can't seem to put out one and not be bombarded with calls directly after. I just don't use them that frequently. I may run a couple about every six or so months. At a normal cost of under $4.00 per sign, they are one of the best real estate advertising and promoting tools accessible. Check the net for sign makers for discount signage costs. I use 18 x 24 signs and set them at high traffic intersections around the town I wish to buy houses in. I additionally position a sign in the front yard following acquiring any house..

You can either use wood stakes or the wire stakes with your signs. I like the wood stakes since they don't twist like the wire ones. Likewise, they are all the more affordable and you can discover pretty much any sensibly measured stick of wood or stake at your neighborhood home improvement shop for a great price. Simply get long lengths and trim down to fit. Then nail the sign to it with the nails with the orange or green plastic tops or you can use screws. There are numerous variations on what the wording on the sign can say. Remember that traffic will move so you need to keep your message short and straightforward so it can be easily understood or caught. Also your phone number must be clear, enormous and simple to peruse.

If you search for my own signs, you will find that it is same likeness to my paper promotion. I like to ensure that I stand out and that all I maintain uniformity across all my promotional endeavors. You need to have something that pops, so a white sign with dull blue letters, or something quite similar, generally is the best draw. Do not worry too much about any of this as often times it's what or how you state it but rather that you're out there promoting and putting out signs. You'll fabricate a 'brand image' after some time if remain constant and legitimate with your estate promotional attempts. When managing advertisement signs, be certain that you take care of any local permission that you require from the government agency in your area. In certain territories or areas they can careless about them, however, in others they can be either issue you tickets or pull the signs down if you do not get the right permissions. In some areas, you may even have to worry about the size of the signs that you will use.

Flyers and Bulletin Board Postings

Flyers and related security are modest methods to get the word out that you are a realtor to purchase property. Simply make a flyer with any of the free online flyer programming telling individuals that you are a real estate agent and how to connect with you. It is best to make multiple flyers advertising your services as this is great marketing. It truly is that simple. At that point, post these flyers on notice boards in your Town or you might want to purchase your property. I also suggest that you place some of them in those plastic sheet shields so rain doesn't destroy them and put them up on telephone posts around neighborhoods possible. . I take a record with me in my vehicle and put them up at whatever point I stop such as the market or any other place. Other examples of places to put them are:

· Laundromats

· Taped up inside public telephones.

· On the counter of any business that will allow you to put them at.

· Bulletin sheets at any area or noteworthy rebate store (heaps of traffic)

· Grocery store declaration sheets

· Fax to mortgage administrators or call them first

These are just various examples. Any place that will allow you to place one there is an ideal location.

Engraved just as Promotional Items

Perfect Real Estate Investor Marketing Ideas - These options ensure that you get top hits on clients who require your Real Estate Investing expertise.

These are a part of my personal options. While they are not the top producers of leads, they will surely make you stand out from the rest.

Pen Knives - These little Swiss knives are the neatest things. They are key chains engraved with your details, mine being: WE BUY HOMES - All cash or expect command over portions inside 24 hours! Call xxx-xxx-xxx I give one of these to somebody so they can keep it and in case they envision selling, they will think about me. They are about $1.75 each.

Key Chains - I offer these to all of my buyers with the keys to their new house on them and also leave them all over the place. They come in the shape of a house or #1 or whatever style you like and have your message on them. You can consider what mine says. Cost - about $.25 cents each.

Pens – I always use these. Whenever I sign a business receipt or anything, I leave my pen. I can't uncover to you what number of fusses I have gotten off of these things and since I routinely need one, I generally have one to give away. My legal counselor even has a store on his end table. I have two types printed: One for sellers says, "We Buy Homes!" and one for buyers says, "Everyone Qualifies." Cost - about $.26 pennies per unit.

Coin Holders - These you hardly locate any more, so everyone gets stunned when I have them. I leave these things everywhere. Mine are yellow with blue letters and my message. Cost - about $.30 pennies each.

I leave these unique things everywhere. I look at it in this way: if I give away 100 pens, 50 sharp edges and 50 coin holders a month, that is basically over $100 bucks a month. That is so far unobtrusive promoting. Furthermore, with the money you can make in a deal, it is a 'no cost' advertising strategy. You can get any of these constrained time promoting items in large quantities.

Business Cards

I order business cards by the 1000's and you should too. There are a huge number of great sellers online that you can purchase your cards from. Business cards are unassuming, and cost about $50.00 for 2000. I leave my cards everywhere, in pay-phones, on bistro tables, my kids even have their own stock to give out. The card shouldn't be too busy, the simpler the better.

There are various conditions of promoting and advertising. Some I have attempted previously, for instance, announcements, door stoppers, professional listing, and TV and radio adverts. I even have a advertising board, an old SUV painted yellow with blue words - WE BUY HOUSES! And my telephone number - that I drive around and park medium-term at special spots. It brings in the calls! Get the advertising going and let the world know who to call when they have a house to sel. If that phone isn't ringing, you aren't benefitting so you need to get a good advertising strategy going and stick with it!

Rob Norquist, a real estate broker surrenders that Newport Beach is as unique as it used to be, with some incredible record bargains. He furthermore agrees with the way that a property, should never be considered reproached, and as a vendor, you should never give up and use the low-end cost. The realities exhibit that, during a particular time period, dependent upon the property features, client's needs, property trades, there may be minutes when a property's estimation drops, yet not forever.

Distinctive urban territories, for instance, Huntington Beach, Costa Mesa, Irvine or Mission Viejo - are considered among 25 other urban zones like the ones with the best land property estimations, with typical estimations of $680,000 and above. The national average in 2007 was $194,300.

Regardless, some property estimations rely upon answers from occupants living in a particular area, so the given numbers, may not always hold tight hence it's always best to wait on a certified appreciation.

In spite of the way that a couple of structures, for instance, Orange County properties, reduced in value in 2007, but they recovered incredibly well after. So this is another driving force as to why as a seller, you should never fear a brief drop, since it is common now and again.

For instance, about 81% of owners, vendors, and realtors, in 2007 trusted that their estate property estimations were over $1 million, against 75% in 2006. So things are beneficial and there is no uncertainty that things change but will level out again, most home owners have finally developed an understanding about what this business is about in this regard. It takes a lot of industriousness and ability to keep up your property's estimation among top ones to ashore grandstand.

Regardless, Norquist, accepts that various Newport Beach disputes are near the end, proceeding with that this city has persevere through the "lodging hang" better than other regions. In any case, the alarming shock attacked more on arrangements, which he surrenders that they are on a falling edge right now, yet there is still trust in better ahead.

Newport Beach is entirely outstanding for its well sought-after properties in the U.S., being a perfect spot for property investment. It's region and closeness to the water, and the beach front view draws investors to the area. Sell-offs around there are uncommonly charming and the people who are enthused about property investment should never miss them.

Experienced real estate agents or even colleagues will certainly caution you that as a buyer you are most likely going to go over various run down properties having possibly no equity, being over assessed. Pros will recognize a the potential in this type of property. So you get in the trades strategy. As a sign, when you comprehend the issue of overestimation, you have to grasp this. Some sellers think the property's estimation, and think they can get above and beyond what it's worth and they will hike up the price on the property. So watch out! The course of action can transform into a problematic system especially when reasonable terms are not agreed by the different sides: owner and buyer. Game plans can happen subtly or with no attempt at being subtle, where land deals come in the picture. Clearly, a property closeout is more secure and more trustful than a private one. Private dealings happen especially when the administrator is a dear friend or close with buyer's, and because of the situation a couple of what is expected in the sale of the property process may be skipped. So in conditions like these, be careful.

Surely, even as a friend, for a real estate agent, money affect things, and can strain relationships after. Clearly, during such a trade, there can be all sort of issues. Moreover, time is a huge issue when land deals are incorporated. If all else fails, and as a brief for a potential buyer, trade method should not be loosened up on a huge stretch of time, in light of the fact that, as I said already, in time, land properties drop their characteristics, and the clients have bit of leeway to purchase it. For this circumstance, not solely does the buyer get affected but the land value too. Why? Because if a property's estimation drops, the cost must drop as well, in case you ever need to sell it again. This is the explanation short arrangements are preferred. Various Realtors, and clients started using this philosophy, since they stood up to the issue as for their property's value. So they picked the selling method that should not take exorbitantly long.

Another noteworthy issue suggests the striking "accelerating clause" which is an official term in real estate as it relates to mortgage. It infers that the bank, after the land property is sold, can demand the portion of the remainder of the money borrowed if the owner defaults on the loan. Realtors can give more information about this. Buying a property which has viably a home loan addresses a completely raised risk. Why? Since, if the home loan was contracted for quite a while, dependent upon the financing costs, and business focus improvement, you may pay the house's far more that the property is worth in the end. In any case, if you have association in watching the business focus, and find a right moment when each interest's value drops, you could allow it to full scale. It's kind of a wagering around here, and realtors, or individual real estate agents acknowledge it best.

Realtors and real estate professionals are here on the property platform, to empower clients to perceive how they can value their homes, what should they look for when trying to sell or buy a house, how to orchestrate, and how to win property trade. Some may express that acquiring or selling a land property is straightforward, yet the reality of the situation is that assessing a house is a problematic strategy. Various real estate professionals, traders, have persevered through various fall-throughs before their first deal, so don't envision that their action ought to be a straightforward one.

Incredibly, a concerning cost and arrangements augmentations of these earlier years have chosen a great part of the time halting the land business. Various real estate professionals who have seen the future needed to achieve something other than what's expected than property business. The credit market is in like manner in a fundamental circumstance, a similar number of Realtors have viewed. Home loan lenders are also a result of land market position right now. Property investment related experts have diminished their help number to land deals, as a sign they have seen it too.

Land has reliably been known as the most secure of investments.

In reality, land theory completed after real assessment into and appraisal of the property (to choose genuine and future worth), can provoke huge advantage.

This is one clarification various people pick land adventure as their line of work.

CHAPTER TWO

A SOLID PLAN FOR GETTING STARTED, EVEN WITH LIMITED CAPITAL

◆ ◆ ◆

There are many approaches to profit in real estate, yet putting resources into rental properties is by a long shot the most worthwhile, offering investors a twofold investment return; an unfaltering leftover pay from the month to month rental and the value from the property itself. Building wealth from rental property investments ought not to be taken lightly. There are numerous interesting points before you buy your first property.

Search for properties that will require practically zero repairs to prepare it for lease, down time means that you will have no salary from the property until it is leased. It is likewise imperative to utilize an accounting report for every property that you mean to lease. This will help you keep track of the amount of resources you have put into the cost of the property and the repairs with the measure of return you can expect once the property is leased. Everything about your investment methodology ought to be all arranged with consideration regarding the everyday management and upkeep just as rental contracts. It is a smart idea to have a list of qualified contractors (plumbers, electricians, decorator etc.) to deal with any potential crisis circumstance. Knowing contractors and what their services cost in that particular area will give you an idea of how profitable the area is and this information will enable you to decide whether the area is right for you.

Properties in well-known areas have the potential for higher rental rates and could likewise be leased week after week. Another incredible rental investment thought is business property - rental rates are quite often higher for this sort of property and most rentals of this sort require a long-term contracts. Consider every conceivable rental property you see with its general potential for quick profit, and ask yourself; is this a perfect area for such a property? How quickly can this property be ready to lease? What is the aggregate sum I should invest, and how much profit can I make on my investment?

When you plan on acquiring your first rental property on credit, at that point you should build up a spreadsheet for the property you aim to buy. A regular spreadsheet will cover a year's course of events and incorporate all costs associated with the property; the greater part of this data can be found in your own financial record you made for the property. Alongside your spreadsheet, you should have a field-tested strategy that outlines your proposition to buy and keep up your rental property. Your strategy ought to incorporate the sort of property you intend to lease, how you plan to oversee and maintain your property and make sure to incorporate any data that demonstrates your capabilities to be productive; a prevalent regular area or high traffic business or business property or other rental property with a high benefit potential. You will also need to incorporate how you expect to defeat any potential hindrances. Putting resources into rental properties for learners is a meaningful way to accomplishing a long-term income.

To have a substantial investment from your rental properties, powerful rental management is vital. The most significant activity for property owners and realtors is to keep the property in brilliant condition. Rental and property management may appear to be straightforward, however, it really requires fastidious thought and diligent work. Realtors may enlist an expert management firm to do all the diligent work or they can do it without anyone else's help.

Owners ought to recall that before leasing the property, they must guarantee that the spot is clean and good. Doing this draws new interest and request in potential tenants and fills in as a code of prohibitive consideration for occupants to be mindful of when living in the owner's property. In addition, they should ensure that there are no harms, glitches or breakdowns on machines, power and water sources. It's prudent to take pictures of each room from each point, so they will fill in as references in the event of any harms.

At the point when occupants are living in a property, it's significant for property owners to be mindful and auspicious in addressing the inhabitant's requests and concerns, once these concerns are reasonable enough. They are additionally obliged to do property assessments for any fundamental fixes and should the property require improvement.

When the occupants have moved away, owners should ensure that there's no damage to the property and that it has been left in a similar condition from the beginning. This makes it easier for them to get the property set and sorted out before the next occupant moves in. In the circumstance of any significant damage, property owners reserve the privilege to request the additional cost from the inhabitants. Ensure that rental properties are profoundly basic for investment benefits.

In the event that property owners hand over their rental properties to real estate agents, they won't need to be disturbed by rental support and management employments in light of the fact that a realtor will take care of all the fundamental managements for them. Their obligations and duties just focus on overseeing and looking after properties, keep the property occupied with persons paying the most for lease and to discover appropriate tenants that would think about the property seriously.

It's essential to obtain the best benefits from any rental property. So realtors and property owners ought to have the correct information and aptitude in overseeing and keeping up their rental properties in great condition.

Benefits of Rental Property Investment

With such a large number of possibilities associated with owning rental property, just as property management, an ever-increasing number of individuals are exploiting this investment. One of the significant focal points to owning rental property is that when you make this kind of investment, you have a substantial resource, as opposed to different sorts of investments, for example, stocks and bonds. In this case, it is clearer the genuine worth of your advantage when you can really observe it. Moreover, the standard rental salary that you get is effectively quantifiable and you can ordinarily anticipate that it should proceed for quite a while.

A few people are worried about putting their cash into budgetary frameworks, so as to develop your riches and resource base. Real estate investment is an incredible arrangement. The securities exchange is known to be very flighty, with continuous vacillations. Actually, real estate will in general remain genuinely solid, notwithstanding when the investment market debilitates to some degree. One reason that real estate keeps on being a wise investment even in a more fragile economy is that it frequently keeps numerous individuals from having the option to acquire a home loan thus increasing the gathering of leaseholders to browse, since despite everything they need a safe place to live.

Rental property can deliver a regular income, which is a favorable position for some individuals. In spite of the fact that you do need to deduct the home loan installment from the rent, you can still earn a profit.

Real estate can acknowledge in worth, contingent upon the market. After some time, numerous properties will wind up being worth more. However, this isn't really a certification yet is reliant on numerous variables, including area, kind and period of property, upkeep and different components. Putting resources into a steady territory will build the chances that your property will acknowledge in worth.

Influence alludes to the capacity to buy rental property by utilizing cash that is obtained. When you can get the cash, you can stand to contribute more since you just need to put down a level of the all-out expense. Since the property itself will verify the obligation, and the rental salary will cover the home loan and duty costs, you remain to make bigger benefits.

Another bit of leeway to rental property is that you can take many expense discussion identified with it. You can deduct the expense of upkeep and fixes, enhancements, charges, protection, contract interest and the sky is the limit from there.

When you have rental property, it is where you can work for yourself. This is a preferred position that many find alluring. Regardless of whether you are proposing to be a low maintenance landowner or build up a profession in property management, you will profit by the capacity to settle on the major choices and experience the autonomy of owning your very own business.

Real Estate Investing: Buying and Selling at the Right Time

Real estate contributing could be summed up as "area, area, area," however, similarly is the planning and timing.

Timing is particularly significant in real estate contributing in light of the fact that:

1. Exchanges can take quite a while, which requires arranging and premonition.

2. All real estate, in all business sectors, are remarkable, with dynamic and rapidly evolving powers.

Since purchasing or selling real estate is a complex and tedious procedure, you have to start it off at the earliest opportunity. While you're trusting that the majority of the pieces will set up, the market can change, leaving you with botched chances for higher benefits. You should most likely prepare and see future valleys and tops in the real estate valuing to realize when to begin purchasing and when to begin selling.

Fixer upper properties can generally win you a decent benefit. That is on the grounds that essential fixes and support can expand a property's estimation by over 10%. On the off chance that you can do the fixes yourself, that is essentially beneficial. You can likewise inquire about abandonment closeouts and houses that are headed to defaulting. In the event that you can strike on a decent property rapidly, you'll get it for less. What's more, in the event that you get the planning perfectly with your examination, you can discover an area on its approach to revitalization and see tremendous future cost increments. Neighborhood governments can likewise offer motivating forces for such territories as they have an enthusiasm for seeing it improve also.

In any case, to have the option to consummate that planning and exploit the above real estate, you need capital close by. This implies you generally need financing close by. That doesn't need to be enormous totals of cash in your investment account. It can be strong credit, endorsed financing from banks and knowing the choices and breaking points for advances that you could get. At the point when different markets endure, savvy real estate contribution can generally make a benefit. You simply need to do the majority of your exploration and ideal the specialty of timing.

The Biggest Mistake: Having an Unclear Property Investment Strategy

At the point when asked by anybody how to put resources into property, I react with a progression of inquiries:

- What are your money related points? At the end of the day, what are you after? Is it true that you are looking for a salary, capital or both?

There is a major contrast between needing to resign in 2 years so you can live off your investment salary and needing to assist your youngsters with educational cost in 12 years.

- Will you have to acquire cash and what amount of risk would you say you will take?
- Will you think about contributing abroad? If yes, where will you contribute - Europe, the Far East or the Middle East?
- What level of risk would you say you will take?
- What occurs in the event that you need your cash back rapidly?

Keep in mind, liquidity is a noteworthy issue in property investment. In the event that you put resources into the stocks and offer market, you can get the telephone and sell in minutes. That is liquidity. Simply have a go at doing that with property and you'll see that it's a totally unique story.

- What about your assessment risk and what might occur in the event that everything turns out badly?
- Do you need to put resources into business or private? Do you by any chance know the distinction?

These are the sort of inquiries you ought to present yourself before you make a plunge and put resources into property. It's exceptionally useful to record your explanations behind needing to put resources into property. You can generally reconsider your rundown on the off chance that you alter your perspective on your investment intentions. In any case, I promise you won't be upset for investing a little energy in upgrading the rundown. Then again, in case you can't concoct any inspiring components for contributing, you're likewise setting yourself up for disappointment. This may appear to be a great deal of work. However, it's a significant piece of the procedure on the off chance that you need to succeed. Keep in mind: purchasing property BEGINS with an all-around idea out arrangement for your leave procedure!

You ought to likewise know about the serious promoting publicity of numerous online real estate operator locations; they regularly go after simple, ignorant people. Be mindful so as not to fall for the promotion with respect to the off arrangements advertised in almost every nation. Media, for example, lustrous abroad magazines that publicize second homes available to be purchased as investments are frequently deceptive.

Another expression of alert - don't be tricked or conned by the guarantees of "make easy money" property plans. Property is a long-term investment. It's anything but difficult to dismiss this as you hear any number of various, new and potentially all the more energizing property investment techniques that give off an impression of profiting NOW. A long time ago, you could buy sensibly evaluated property, lease it out and take in substantial income in a moderately brief timeframe. Be that as it may, circumstances are different and this is not true anymore.

Not all real estate operators will be forthright about this reality. In the same way as others, you may erroneously expect that your real estate operator is resolved to allow you to get the most ideal return for your cash. Tragically, this is frequently not the situation. The fundamental objective of real estate operators is to sell property - period. Do you think it is to their greatest advantage to persuade you to make long-term property investments? Certainly not!

Media assets can likewise hamper your property investment openings by composing terrible or great reports about property investments that essentially aren't valid. Property-related columnists are being paid to compose about the real estate showcase or rewarding investment openings. Publicizing is enormous business and columnists might be paid to compose a shining report about different abroad or neighborhood investments that is totally false. Thus, it's ideal to disregard most of what you read in the magazines and direct some strong statistical surveying alone. All things considered, it's your cash, so you need to contribute to it wisely!

Luckily, there are some solid assets accessible to enable you to find out about current patterns in the property showcase.

Also, make certain to converse with nearby real estate operators just as some dependable rental management organizations. They can talk about a portion of the more fruitful nearby investment property methodologies. Remember individuals from your neighborhood business network and retailers in your locale. They can prove to be priceless sources of data with regards to neighborhood property investment.

If you set up clear investment targets, you can concentrate just on the applicable kinds of property. I don't prescribe picking in excess of two property types in case you're an amateur property investor. Given the huge measure of conceivable investment properties, this little advance can spare you a great deal of squandered hours. You ought to consider the urban communities. You would then be able to decide the best and most exceedingly awful investment territories of a particular city by dissecting different factors, for example, wrongdoing and business measurements.

The main concern is, don't depend on just the most recent investment trends to figure out where to contribute your cash. This can prove to be an expensive error, particularly on the off chance that you are new to property investment. Invest some energy, deciding your rousing elements for contributing, ask yourself a few significant questions and limit your objective territory to a couple of urban communities. These will significantly improve your opportunity of accomplishment. With a touch of arranging and exhortation, you can build up a reasonable investment procedure and maintain a strategic distance from the most widely recognized property investments.

The most effective method to Begin a Real Estate Business: With Little or No Money

The real estate part is a flourishing one. Many make investments by purchasing terrains and building houses to be set up for rent. Obviously, the most ideal approach to be a part of it is to have cash for buys. Notwithstanding, you can presently purchase properties without having money. In spite of the fact that without cash, something still should be advertised, it could be your time, your ability or your range of abilities. Indeed, there are bargains that should be possible without you having cash. How?

Accomplice

In the event that you have enormous ideas, solid field-tested strategy and an incredible reputation, at that point you can get an accomplice who has what you don't – cash. The individual can give the financing while you remain on the overseeing part of the business. You ought to also talk about how benefits will be shared. Make it a success win for your accomplices and get it going.

Another type of joining forces is by contributing with a structure temporary worker. In the case that you do not have a few abilities, for example, carpentry and pipes aptitudes, to fix up and exchange a property, you can join forces with somebody who has these abilities and could help with the initial installment. When you make a benefit on the deal, you will have the upfront installment for your next real estate investment.

Converse with individuals

There is no cash expected to get it under contract or finding bargains for investors. You can help individuals discover bargains. At that point, you can have individuals who will subsidize your arrangement, or even better, you may have bit by bit made cash to purchase your own property.

Get cash from family or companions

On the off chance that you have no cash to begin your real estate business, obtaining cash from family and companions is another alternative that you can utilize. This might be less formal, however, make certain to give them an authority promissory note with installment due dates, a particular financing cost, and what ownership, assuming any, the bank will have on the property. Keeping your assertion is significant as it might decide how they will get you in the event that you have a comparative need later on. In the event that you pay back the credit on schedule and with interest, these loan specialists may be eager to loan to you again for future tasks. This is an extraordinary choice, yet numerous connections have been pulverized on the grounds that they didn't deal with the procedures included appropriately.

Work out an exchange

You can pay for real estate by giving the required/particular ability you have. For instance, a temporary worker could offer a real estate designer work in return for an upfront installment.

Search for frantic merchants

These individuals are frantic to sell for reasons, such as, insolvency, separate, the demise of a relative, a new position, poor state of the property and so on. They are generally all the more ready to give financing to make it all work out rapidly.

Investigate vender financing

On the off chance that the vender is inspired enough, they might be happy to make it simple for you to buy by giving you an advance. You could offer to make higher, regularly scheduled installments rather than an initial installment. You could also create an arrangement where the dealer pays your upfront installment to the purchaser so as to sell the property quicker. The merchant may anticipate that you should pay him/her back or s/he may toss the upfront installment in for nothing, basically bringing down the selling cost.

Whatever you choose to do, ensure you get a real estate lawyer to review the understanding with the goal that the two gatherings are secured.

CHAPTER THREE

IMPORTANT THINGS TO NOTE WHILE EMBARKING ON A REAL ESTATE BUSINESS

◆ ◆ ◆

With regards to selling real estate, there are some major hints you may have to ponder when doing as such. The rationalization is - in case you are attempting to extricate as much as you can from your property, there are certain things you may have to think about so as to increase your chances as a vender. Here we're going to address some significant parts of selling real estate which relate to area, inspiration, nation of your home, and in the end, the fee you will be okay with. Subsequent to perusing the information given here, you may have a most suitable comprehension about promoting your property and why each and every one of these views will be critical.

Area

Understand that location had a remarkable deal to do with the motivation behind why you bought your property in any case. Similarly, as it was once widespread at that point, it winds up huge when it is a perfect opportunity to sell. Area will have a lot to do with the new purchaser's choice simply as the price in which you will sense right with as soon as the property is sold. In this way, you'll have to mull over the place when you are making ready your property, arranging the inside, and estimating it as per the present market esteem.

Inspiration

You'll have to ask yourself, 'What is the reason for promoting this property? Are you inclined to take the necessary steps to get your property sold? Is it real that you are going to battle for each nickel and dime or would you say you will be pleased to arrange a couple of hundred greenbacks anywhere?' Your inspiration will decide if your property gets sold. In the case that you are not a roused vender, the odds are you'll be clutching that property for a lengthy while.

Condition

The state of your property is essential with regards to the enthusiasm of new purchasers. Your property ought to be prepared so that it shows the outside, the inside, the apparatuses, and the kitchen and washroom specifically. You should knock up the bargaining offer by making certain you deal with the right finishing. Paint the backyard each time required, clean or supplant covers as required, paint the internal if necessary, and make sure that the kitchen and restroom are in tip pinnacle condition. You'll likewise want to listen on evacuating any messiness that may want to make the inside of the home seems to be littler than it as of now is.

Cost

Cost will be in a similar way as tremendous as the area, the notion for selling and the country of your home. The cost of your home should be founded on relative prices inside your zone. Perhaps the most perfect strategies to price your property will be to speak with a real estate expert who is very trained about your place and the fluctuating costs. They will have the alternative to help you with market patterns or anything that would possibly have an effect on charges on a property of your size.

These are just a couple of widespread suggestions that ought to be considered as when promoting real estate. If you are in an area that you are encountering inconvenience with regards to selling your home, you might want to pick the administrations given by using a real estate professional that has legitimate mastering of the kind of property you have, and the specific vicinity where you intend to sell.

When you lease a room through real estate, your notoriety is fundamentally significant. That is in reality why you have to assurance that the room is completely ideal and fit as a fiddle.

Real estate is quite energizing stuff. No risk to get around it, this agency is making huge, sizable waves. Why? Real estate is a sizeable site meant to motivate leasing everything from residences and whole condos to private rooms, pontoons and yes even personal islands. There are several motives that this administration is getting on in a noteworthy manner and for this reason, numerous individuals are eager on making use of it.

For explorers, spots to continue to be different than resorts are without a doubt a gift from heaven, as it allows explorers to absolutely sidestep the lodging business. On the off risk that you trust you're the one who has had negative help at a lodging, experienced negative sanitation conditions or encountered a scope of astonishments, for example, loud rooms, thoughtless team of workers or cheating, you are obviously not the only one.

Real estate and one of a kind locales are taking advantage of this and have set out to offer travelers an absolutely first-rate way to deal with motion lodging. Not very shockingly, accommodations and inns are vexed and have gone to campaigning as an instrument for securing their organizations.

The explanation that humans love real estate is that it is currently attainable to rapidly and correctly transform your home into a little cash machine. Barely any individuals will get rich by means of making use of real estate. However, there is surely a respectable arrangement of cash to be made. Since it is attainable to strive and lease a male or female room, any other world has been opened up to explorers hoping to save huge on housing and loan holders, hoping to produce some extra salary.

An ever-growing number of mortgage holders are finding this likelihood and the income that being engaged with the webpage can bring. Nonetheless, it is huge for mortgage holders to recognize that neatness is a major issue the place real estate is concerned. All things considered, purchasers can compose audits and obviously, carry what desires be all through internet based totally life. On the off threat that your residence is dirty or normally unsavory, you will undermine your endeavors. Terrible surveys will price you beyond all doubt as there is a lot of rivalry.

The most perfect strategy to guarantee that your property gives predictable and dependable help and neatness levels is to settle on a specialist and skilled house-keeping administration.

A real estate agency realizes quality how to keep your home as best as should be predicted, underneath the circumstances. Along these lines, you will have the alternative to ensure your notoriety and preserve new traffic wanting invariably and a day.

Owning a bit of property isn't simple because of the nonstop increment of land costs. As simple as it looks, to lease property can be troublesome and unpleasant. There are a ton of factors to consider earlier than when you hire property. These include the rent rate, the landowner's experience, the spot and other things. You have to firstly ask a lot about each one of these things before intending to sign the agreement. Set apart some effort to do all these so as to get the excellent association and the most suitable spot that you and your family can stay in.

Exploring for every other spot to live in can be simple on the off chance that you do your exploration appropriately. In the event that a rental appears wonderful to you, have a go at touring the spot more than a few events in the course of the day, work week and at the end of the week. When you do this, you will have an ordinary thought on the everyday workout routines of your neighbors while concurrently watching their condition. If you are curious about the spot, take anyone with you. It is constantly prudent that you do not visit a property for rent alone. This is for your personal protection, specifically in conditions when you are meeting the landowner himself and no longer a real estate operator.

Contrast the property and the vicinity with your way of life. In the event that you have a vehicle, does the loft have a carport? If not, will you have a spot to stop? Is it located close to a bus station? These are truly very comparable matters you will ask notwithstanding when purchasing a house. See whether or not the property is set to your working environment and generally if transportation prices will be costly.

When you rent property, reflect on what wide variety of stuff you have. Will they all fit in your new residence? On the off threat that you adore pets or in the tournament that you have one, it is perfect to see whether the landowner allows tenants with pets.

One of the most widespread contemplations in property rental is the standard purpose of the spot. Check if there are termites or rodents or some different bugs. In spite of the truth that it isn't your duty to have the condo looking great, it will be less distressing for you in the event that you test for harms, so the landowner will have the option to do a few fixes before you pass in.

One of the most considerable, fascinating points is whether you can control the cost of the hire rate. When you lease property, it is necessary to take note of the fact that all spots for hire no longer have comparable rates. The distinction lies, for the most part, in the territory and offices. Consenting to the terms of installment ought to likewise be investigated. For the most part, a condo is paid month to month, while others demand that they be paid beforehand. Discuss this with the landowner.

To lease property, you must settle on a smart and practicable choice. This may also possibly be in all likelihood the hardest desire to make. Consider each one of the favorable instances just as impediments of the spot before you do what desires to be done.

So, how does the all-cash down procedure work by means of shopping for a property with money? Most importantly, let me repeat that I genuinely didn't have any money. Alternatively, I had a lot of fee from Terry's property and a few houses that I claimed set up collectively to give me a substantial up front installment. Banks and property loan agencies will use well-known cash from a home-value savings extension as money to buy a home. In any event, they did it in 1997, beneath the monetary rules of the day. What you recollect about home loans and loaning is that the regulations trade always, so this gadget I utilized in 1997 ought to perhaps have the alternative to be utilized later on. Regardless of whether or not it is or cannot be utilized again does not commonly make a difference to me, as I accept that there will constantly be a strategy to buy real estate with limited cash down at some point or another. There will persistently be a method to procure real estate, yet precisely how that will be completed later on, I'm not absolutely sure.

I began acquiring residences in the Mayfair vicinity of Philadelphia with the expenses in the $30,000 to $40,000 per home price region. I would purchase a home with three rooms and one restroom on the second floor with a kitchen, lounge area, and the front room on the fundamental floor and a storm cellar. What we call a column home in Philadelphia would consist of a patio out the front and a terrace the width of the home. Most column houses in Philadelphia are below twenty-two feet wide. For those of you who are now not from Philadelphia and cannot picture what a Philadelphia column property resembles, I propose you watch the movie Rocky. Twenty-two properties on every facet of each square will actually take a look at your ability to be a neighbor. Things that will for the most part motivate a contention with your Philadelphia neighbors often originate from stopping, your youngsters climbing, garbage receptacles, parties, and the outward appearance of your home.

In 1998, my better half and I moved in together and to suburbia of Philadelphia known as Warminster. In the wake of residing on an avenue in Tacony, like Rocky did, I surely expected having space between my property and my close by neighbor. I informed Terry not to attempt and think about chatting with the people who lived close by to us. I recommended her if one of them comes over with a nut cake, I am going to take it and punt it like a football without delay into their terrace. My new neighbors in Warminster ended up being outstanding individuals and on the other hand it took me eighteen months before I was able to find that out.

So, you simply purchased your line property for $35,000 in Mayfair, and after $2000 in closing charges and $5000 in restoration costs, you get yourself a first-rate occupant who wishes to rent the home. Subsequent to leasing the property with fine earnings of $200 every month, you nowadays have a tremendous responsibility of $42,000 on your home fee deposit extension that should be satisfied. When acquiring the home, I didn't get a home loan as I just bought a home for cash as it is stated in the business. All monies I spent on this residence have been spent from the home-value credit score extension.

The cross presently is to satisfy your home-value credit score extension so you can go do it once more. We currently go to a manipulate an account with your repaired property and tell the property mortgage division that you need to do a cash out renegotiating of your real estate venture. It clarifies that the neighborhood you purchase your property in ought to have a greater sizable scope of estimating as the region of Mayfair did in the mid-90s. The estimating of homes in Mayfair is very bizarre as you would see a $3000 contrast in home estimations starting with one rectangular then onto the next. This used to be enormous when doing a cash out renegotiating in light of the truth that it is pretty easy for the financial institution to see that I simply bought my property for $35,000, paying little idea to the way that I did numerous fixes. I should legitimize the way that I've spent greater money on my property to set it up and by getting a tenant in, it used to be currently a recommended bit of real estate from a task angle.

In the event that I was once lucky like I used to be in many events, over doing this arrangement of acquiring houses in Mayfair and the appraiser would make use of houses a rectangular or two away and return with an examination of $45,000. In those days there had been initiatives enabling a financial specialist to purchase a property for 10 percentage down or left in as cost doing a ninety percent cash out renegotiate, giving me lower back commonly $40,500. Using this gadget enabled me to get back the enormous majority of the cash I put down on the property. I in fact paid solely $1,500 down for this new home. For what reason did the property loan corporations and the appraisers continue giving me the numbers I needed? I would simply recommend the financial institution I want this to come in at $45,000 or I am clearly retaining it as financed as it stands. They commonly regarded to give me what I needed, sensibly speaking.

This complete manner took three to 4 months, during which time I have also spared a couple of thousand dollars. Between the money I spared from my undertaking and my investments and money out renegotiating, I had recharged majority of my assets from my home-value credit score extension that used to be present, to begin the method once more. Furthermore, that is simply what I proposed to do. I utilized this framework to buy four to six properties a year, using a similar cash to purchase home after property after property once more and again. In all actuality, the approach is a no-cash down or minimal expenditure down procedure. At the time, let's say I had $60,000 in reachable belongings to use to buy houses off of my HELOC, I would purchase a home and afterward renew the cash. It used to be an awesome device that was once legitimate, and I could see my delusion about being a real estate monetary expert drawing near to an inevitable truth that I wasn't there yet.

During the years from 1995 to 2002, the real estate showcase in Philadelphia made innovative increments of possibly 6% as every 12 months went on. I began to observe my complete belongings that used to be 100 percentage value, which I had no exclusive types of investments to see when computing my complete assets. As a rule, the initial five years of my real estate vocation turned out poorly in light of the lousy selections I made while shopping for buildings and the decrease in the market. Moreover, my absence of gaining knowledge of and involvement in fixes made it an unpleasant. I bolstered myself essentially through my vocation as an income rep. Alternatively, I may want to apprehend what would be inevitable that not some distance off, real estate would have been my full-time gig.

Realty Professionals of America

I declare a vicinity of enterprise that has a real estate organization as an inhabitant referred to as Realty Professionals of America. The organization has a remarkable association where another operator receives 75 percent of the commission and the agent receives simply 25%. If you don't have any acquaintance with it, this is quite a first-rate arrangement, especially for any other real estate specialist. The organization additionally presents a 5% sponsorship charge to the specialist who consumers them on every arrangement they do. In the case where you send a man or woman who is a real estate professional in to the employer that you have supported, the professional will pay you a 5 % sponsorship out of the representative's end. So, the new real property agent you supported can at present achieve seventy-five percent commissions. Notwithstanding the abovementioned, Realty Professionals of America seek to construct the real estate professional's bonus by means of 5% subsequent to accomplishing mixture fee benchmarks, up to a restriction of ninety percent. When a commission benchmark is agreed on, an operator's bonus fee is possibly diminished if commissions in the subsequent year do not arrive at a lower sum. I, as of now, hold 85% of each and every one of my arrangements' bonuses. In addition to that, I get sponsorship assessments of 5 % from the commissions that the operators I supported procure. On the off threat that you'll like to become familiar with being supported into Realty Professionals of America's incredible arrangement, it would be perfect if you call me straightforwardly at 267-988-2000.

Getting My Real Estate License

Something that I did in the late spring of 2005 in the wake of leaving my all-day occupation was once to make preparations to get my real estate permit. Getting my real estate permit used to be something I continuously needed to do. However, I never seemed to have the possibility to do it. I'm sure you have heard that motive a thousand times. Individuals constantly state that they will accomplish something soon as they discover a chance to do it. Then again, they never appear to discover the time, isn't always that right? I do whatever it takes not to force myself to rationalize anything. So, I've determined earlier that I, at any point, left my all-day work that one of the primary matters I would do was to get my real estate permit. I joined up with a college referred to as the American Real Estate Institute for a fourteen-day full-time program to gather my permit to promote real estate in the territory of Pennsylvania. Two persons with a world of experience showed the class, and I delighted in the time I spent there. Following the route at the American Real Estate Institute, I booked the following reachable day supplied through the kingdom to take the test. My instructors' advice to take the check, following the type, ended up being an exceptional proposal. I finished the check decisively and have utilized my permit ordinarily to purchase real estate and minimize the costs. If you wish to be a full-time real estate monetary specialist or a commercial enterprise real estate investor, you need to get a permit. While I know a couple of persons who don't accept this, I'm persuaded it's the major way.

I took a shot at one association at $3 million. The fee to the purchaser's real estate operator used to be $75,000. When my provider took an offer, I walked with $63,000 commission on that association alone. With the everyday rate each and every time of being an actual estate expert running about $1200 each and every year, this one association on my own would've paid for my real estate permit for fifty-three years. Also, the number of incidental advantages like approaching the numerous posting administration supplied to an excessive wide variety of real property sellers in this nation. While there are distinctive methods to gain admittance to a range of posting administrations or another application like it, a real estate permit is a brilliant approach.

An element of the negatives I hear again about having your real estate is the way you need to unveil that you are real professional when buying a property.. On the other hand, I do not think about this to be a negative by any means. In case you're talented in the distinctiveness of exchange, it's in reality one more obstacle that you need to manage. I wager you may want to wind up in a claim where a court could accept in light of the fact that you are a real property agent, you need to be aware of each one of these things. I do not go through my time on earth, agonizing over the million distinctive ways I can be sued or stress over getting hit by an automobile each time I pass the road.

CHAPTER FOUR

FINDING THE BEST MARKET/PRICE FOR YOUR INVESTMENT PORTFOLIO SHOULD BE FOR YOUR BUDGET

◆ ◆ ◆

Putting resources into Real Estate: The Simple Strategies

Purchasing and owning real estate is an energizing investment procedure that can be both fulfilling and worthwhile. Unlike stock and bond investors, planned real estate owners can utilize influence to purchase a property by paying a segment of the all-out expense in advance, at that point satisfying the parity, in addition to enthusiasm, after some time. While a conventional home loan generally requires a 20% to 25% up front installment, sometimes, a 5% initial installment is everything necessary to buy a whole property. The capacity to control the advantage the minute papers are marked encourages both real estate flippers and landowners, who can thus take out second contracts on their homes, so as to make initial installments on extra properties.

Here are four manners by which investors can put properties to great use:

1. Wanting to be a Landlord

Perfect for: People with DIY and redesign aptitudes, who have the tolerance to oversee inhabitants.

The stuff to Get Started: Substantial capital expected to back direct upkeep expenses and spread over blank months.

Merits: Rental properties can give ordinary pay, while expanding accessible capital through influence. Also, many related costs are charge deductible and any misfortunes can balance gains in different investments.

Demerits: Unless you contract a property management organization, rental properties will in general be filled with consistent migraines. In most pessimistic scenario situations, unruly tenants can destroy property. Besides, in certain rental market atmospheres, a landowner should either suffer opportunities or charge less lease, so as to cover costs until things turn. On the other side, when the home loan has been satisfied totally, most of the lease turns into all benefit.

Obviously, rental salary is anything but a landowner's sole core interest. In a perfect circumstance, a property increases in value through the span of the home loan, leaving the landowner with a more significant resource than he began with.

2. Real Estate Investment Groups

Perfect for: People who need to claim rental real estate without the problems of running it.

The stuff to Get Started: A capital pad and access to financing.

Merits: This is a considerably more distant way to deal with real estate that still gives pay and appreciation.

Demerits: There is an opening danger with real estate investment gatherings, regardless of whether it's spread over the gathering or whether it's owner explicit. Moreover, management overhead can eat into returns.

Real estate investment gatherings resemble little common supports that put resources into rental properties. In a commonplace real estate investment gathering, an organization purchases or constructs a lot of loft squares or apartment suites. Investors are then able to buy them through the organization, along these lines joining the gathering. A solitary investor can possess one or numerous units of independent living space, yet the organization working the investment bunch on the whole, deals with the majority of the units, taking care of upkeep, publicizing opportunities and meeting inhabitants. In return for leading these management assignments, the organization takes a month to month lease.

A standard real estate investment gathering lease is in the investor's name and the majority of the units form a part of the lease to make preparations for intermittent opportunities. To this end, you'll get some pay regardless of whether your unit is vacant. For whatever length of time that the opening rate for the pooled units doesn't spike excessively high, there ought to be enough to take care of expenses.

While these gatherings are hypothetically protected approaches to put into real estate, they are powerless against similar expenses that frequent the shared store industry. Besides, these gatherings are private investments where deceitful management groups bilk investors out of their cash. Demanding due perseverance is in this way basic to sourcing the best chances.

3. Real Estate Trading

Perfect for: People with noteworthy involvement in real estate valuation and advertising.

The stuff to Get Started: Capital and the capacity to do or administer fixes as required.

Merits: Real estate exchanging has a shorter timespan during which capital and exertion are tied up in a property. In any case, contingent upon economic situations, there can be huge returns, even in shorter time allotments.

Demerits: Real estate exchanging requires a more profound market information matched with karma. Hot markets can cool out of the blue, leaving transient merchants with misfortunes or long-term pains.

Real estate exchanging is the wild side of real estate investment. Similarly as informal investors are an alternate creature from purchase and hold investors, real estate merchants are particular from purchase and lease landowners. A valid example: real estate merchants regularly look to beneficially sell the underestimated properties they purchase, in only three to four months. Unadulterated property flippers regularly don't put resources into improving properties. In this manner, investment should, as of now, have the characteristic worth expected to turn a benefit with no adjustments or they'll kill the property from dispute.

Flippers who can't quickly empty a property may end up in a difficult situation, since they ordinarily don't keep enough uncertain money close by to pay the home loan on a property, over the long-term. This can prompt continued misfortunes. There is an entire other sort of flipper who makes cash by purchasing sensibly estimated properties, including an incentive by remodeling them. This can be a more drawn out term investment, where investors can just stand to take on each or two properties in turn.

4. Real Estate Investment Trusts (REITs)

Perfect for: Investors who need portfolio presentation to real estate without a customary real estate exchange.

The stuff to Get Started: Investment capital.

Merits: REITs are basically profit paying stocks whose center property contain business real estate properties with long-term, money delivering leases.

Demerits: REITs are basically stocks, so the influence related with customary rental real estate does not have any significant bearing.

A REIT is made when a company (or trust) utilizes investors' cash to buy and work salary properties. REITs are purchased and sold on the real trades, similar to some other stock. A partnership must compensate out 90% of its assessable benefits as profits, so as to keep up its REIT status. By doing this, REITs abstain from making good on corporate salary regulatory expense, while a customary organization would be saddled on its benefits and afterward need to choose whether or not to appropriate its after-charge benefits as profits.

Like ordinary profit paying stocks, REITs are a strong investment for securities exchange investors who want customary pay. In contrast to the previously mentioned sorts of real estate investment, REITs bear the cost of investors' entrée into nonresidential investments. For example, shopping centers or places of business, which are commonly not achievable for individual investors to buy legitimately. All the more significantly, REITs are profoundly fluid since they are trade exchanged. As it were, you won't require a realtor and a title move to enable you to cash out your investment. REITs are a progressively formalized adaptation of a real estate investment gathering.

At long last, when taking a look at REITs, investors ought to recognize value REITs that possess structures, and home loan REITs that give financing to real estate and fiddle with home loan supported protections (MBS). Both offer introduction to real estate; however, the idea of the presentation is unique. A value REIT is progressively customary, in that it speaks to ownership in real estate, while the home loan REITs center around the pay from home loan financing of real estate.

Regardless of whether real estate investors utilize their properties to produce rental pay or to wait for their chance until the ideal selling opportunity emerges, it's possible to work out a hearty investment program by paying a generally little piece of a property's all out an incentive in advance. In any case, likewise with any investment, there is benefit and potential inside real estate, regardless of whether the general market is up or down.

Tips for Diversifying Your Portfolio

At the point when the market is blasting, it appears to be practically difficult to sell a stock for any sum; not exactly the cost at which you got it. But since we can never make sure of what the market will do at any minute, we can't overlook the significance of a well-differentiated portfolio in any economic situation.

What Is Diversification?

Diversification is a call to war for some, budgetary organizers, subsidize supervisors and individual investors the same. It is a management procedure that mixes various investments in a solitary portfolio. The thought behind expansion is that an assortment of investments will yield a higher return. It likewise recommends that investors will face lower risks by putting resources into various vehicles.

Figure out how to Practice Disciplined Investing

Expansion is certifiably not another idea. With the advantage of knowing the past, we can set back and investigate the responses of the business sectors as they staggered during the dotcom crash and again during the Great Recession.

We ought to recall that contributing is an artistic expression, not an automatic response, so an opportunity to practice trained contributing with an enhanced portfolio is before expansion turns into a need. When a normal investor "responds" to the market, 80% of the harm is as of now done. Here, more than most places, a great offense is your best safeguard and a well-enhanced portfolio joined with an investment more than five years can weather any storm.

Here are five hints for helping you with expansion:

1. Spread the Riches

Values can be magnificent, yet don't place the majority of your cash in one stock or one part. Consider making your very own virtual common store by putting resources into a bunch of organizations you know, trust and even use in your everyday life.

In any case, stocks aren't only the main interesting point. You can also put resources into items, traded funds (ETFs), and real estate investment trusts (REITs). What's more, don't simply adhere to your own command post. Think past it and go worldwide. Along these lines, you'll spread your risks around, which can prompt greater prizes. Individuals will contend that putting resources into what you realize will leave the normal investor also vigorously retail-arranged. Yet knowing an organization or utilizing its products and enterprises, can be a solid and healthy way to deal with this segment.

All things considered, don't fall into the snare of going excessively far. Ensure you hold yourself to a portfolio that is sensible. There's no sense in putting resources into 100 distinct vehicles when you really don't have opportunity or assets to keep up. Attempt to restrict yourself to around 20 to 30 distinct investments.

2. Consider Index or Bond Funds

You might need to consider including list reserves or fixed-pay assets to the mix. Putting resources into protections that track different records makes a superb long-term broadening investment for your portfolio. By including some fixed-pay arrangements, you are further supporting your portfolio against market instability and vulnerability. These assets attempt to coordinate the exhibition of expansive records, as opposed to putting resources into a particular area, they attempt to mirror the security market's worth.

These assets are frequently accompanied by low charges, which is another reward. It implies more cash in your pocket. The management and working expenses are negligible in view of the stuff to run these assets.

3. Continue Building Your Portfolio

Include to your investments a normal premise. In the event that you have $10,000 to contribute, use dollar-cost averaging. This methodology is utilized to help smooth out the pinnacles and valleys made by market instability. The thought behind this technique is to cut down your investment chance by contributing a similar measure of cash over some stretch of time.

With dollar-cost averaging, you put cash all the time into a safe place. Utilizing this system, you'll purchase more offers when costs are low, and less when costs are high.

4. Realize When to Get Out

Purchasing and holding and dollar-cost averaging are sound procedures. Be that as it may, in light of the fact that you have your investments on autopilot doesn't mean you ought to overlook the powers at work.

Remain current with your investments and remain side by side of any adjustments in general economic situations. You'll need to realize what is befalling the organizations you put resources into. Thusly, you'll additionally have the option to advise when it's an ideal opportunity to cut your misfortunes, sell and proceed onward to your next investment.

5. Watch out for Commissions

In the event that you are not the exchanging type, learn what you are getting for the expenses you are paying. A few firms charge a month to month expense, while others charge value-based expenses. These can include and overshadow your primary concern.

Know about what you are paying and what you are getting for it. Keep in mind, the least expensive decision isn't generally the best. Keep yourself refreshed on whether there are any progressions to your expenses.

Relieving Risks: The Real Estate Investments Strategy

The current monetary conditions have made way for exceptional investment openings and furthermore, some difficult snags for both the new and experienced investor. All together for you as a Real Estate Investor to make long-term money related progress, you should execute powerful Risk Mitigation methodologies. The accompanying data will give you procedures you ought to consider as you are assessing potential investment areas and getting and overseeing investment properties.

Perhaps the greatest test investors face today is verifying financing - You should understand the Lenders Underwriting criteria before going into the arrangement. With endorsing rules proceeding to turn out to be progressively prohibitive, you should investigate innovative approaches to get around customary financing. A portion of these strategies incorporate the following:

- Other People's Money (OPM)
- Seller's Financing Hard Money
- Private Money

- Self-Directed IRA's from you or different Investors
- Joint Ventures
- Partnerships

It is extraordinary to persuade the seller to subsidize the arrangement, yet do you have a leave procedure on how you will change from this transient financing? Having the property balanced out during your leave system execution will be basic to verify long-term financing from ordinary lenders.

o Being ready to change yourself in different occasions - What worked a year ago or even a month ago may not work today. For instance, when you glance back at real estate agents and how they worked together in 2006 generally, purchasers would swarm to them and as a rule of an estimated right property, there were offers that may have brought about offering up the business cost. In the present market, with couple of purchasers qualifying for financing, the fruitful agent must have a powerful promoting arrangement to draw in the purchasers in the market. Many have experienced issues with this change and are never again ready to continue themselves in the business.

o Development of a far-reaching business plan - Your business plan is your guide that will lead you towards your investment objectives. Generally, numerous individuals either don't have a business plan or are not utilizing it as the useful asset it may be. Coming up next are some basic components of an effectively actualized business plan:

- Effective objective setting should meet the accompanying "Shrewd" attributes:
- Specific
- Measurable
- Attainable
- Relevant
- Time bound

- High level objectives must stream down to what you ought to chip away at every day. This is a zone where numerous individuals experience difficulty and therefore, get disheartened in accomplishing their objectives.

- The business plan is a living archive that ought to develop with you.

- Your duty to work your business plan is fundamental.

- Understand your dangers and relieve whatever number of them as would be prudent - The present market isn't excusing and on the off chance that you settle on a terrible choice or things go somewhat off track, it could be the part of the bargain.

- Put a solid expert group set up -

- Use them in your everyday business choices; not exactly when it is the ideal opportunity for charges or your need them to audit a deal.

- Have the correct group. Ensure you are utilizing experts who really know your business. I hear so often that individuals are utilizing an inappropriate expert in their group. Because your uncle is an attorney does not mean they have the contributing background that will profit you. Keep in mind when choosing your group, you are talking with them!

- Develop a viable system to help guarantee your long-term achievement -

- Attend investment association occasions. This gives the inspiration numerous individuals need.

- Come to the gatherings early and remain late; this is the place you will get the chance to "work the room".

- Meet whatever number of individuals as could be expected under the circumstances and trade business cards. It will be crucial for you to catch up with these contacts so as to begin to set up an association with them. Keep in mind, every individual you meet has their own system that at last you may access. This is a region I feel numerous individuals battle with. This isn't about what number of business cards you gather and put in a shoebox, it's tied in with creating connections.

- Don't confine your systems administration just to real estate gatherings. There are numerous associations that could benefit you as a real estate investor.

- Prepare yourself with a strong investment instructive establishment - Only through information would you be able to understand how to moderate risk.

- Have a strong resource assurance plan set up - Here is another region numerous investors miss the mark. In these belligerent occasions, you should set up defensive measures so somebody doesn't go along and remove all you have developed.

- Be appropriately safeguarded - Make sure the property use meets the strategy. Continuously consider the most elevated risk inclusion accessible.

What is the least risk plan of action to make long-term riches and income that will support advertise variances? The hold to rent plan of action is an incredible decision; when you consider the gratefulness, income, standard decrease, charge impetuses and the capacity to use your capital, it is clear why probably the best investors are intensely into this model.

Top of the List Risk Mitigations

- Don't utilize the highest point of the market rents when assessing properties - If the property bodes well at 90%, you have a champ. No one can really tell when you may need to limit the lease dependent on an evolving request.

- Calculate execution on the most traditionalist use - If for instance you are concentrating on multi-occupancy residence which normally makes more pay than a solitary family rental, utilize the lower single-family number. I have seen an excessive number of investors buying properties dependent on the multi-occupancy residence model just to find that they couldn't find multi-occupancies and therefore, went topsy-turvy with the property.

- Never consider unlawful condos and the pay it produces when assessing investment choices - One call to the town from a furious neighbor or inhabitant and you are facing potential fines and the evacuation of the illicit loft and occupants. Additionally, remember when you are thinking about illicit use and inhabitance, you are in risk if a protection guarantee is ever documented. Your insurance agency will probably decline to cover the case and that can have an overwhelming effect in the event that somebody gets injured.

- Use traditionalist inhabitance desires - Never utilize the present zone inhabitance rate when assessing investments.

- Has great income - Make sure you are getting adequate income from your properties with the goal of it to support itself monetarily. The exact opposite thing you need is to go into your pockets every month to cover costs. On the off chance for instance, one month costs expend the positive salary you will make throughout the following 4 months, you are putting yourself at incredible monetary risk. We see unreasonably numerous associations offering total bundle bargains at what is, by all accounts, incredible section costs just to discover that towards the part of the bargain you are left with $150! I'm certain you know how effective that can get retained in the event that you needed to get an exchange contractual worker for a normal fix.

- Have great overall revenues in a wholesale or flip arrangement - In a solid seller's market, you can have littler edges when doing a wholesale or flip. In any case, during a buyer's market, bigger edges will be required so as to ensure yourself in the event that you have to limit the business cost.

- Have a solid value position going into an arrangement - Having a solid value position when obtaining a property will enable you to use this value by hauling out capital for some time later. What's more, it will give you a support in the occasion the market brings a down-turn.

- Have satisfactory capital stores - I see such a large number of investors utilizing all their accessible cash-flow to buy the property and to place it in administration without building up any stores. These stores might be vital because of the accompanying circumstances:
- Hold you over during the rent period
- Expected fixes
- Unexpected fixes
- Budget over-runs
- Utility cost development
- Take time to become more acquainted with the individuals you plan on working with - Developing a strong association with the individuals you plan on working with is so significant. Things can turn out badly with business connections from numerous points of view that incorporate the accompanying:
- People who are deliberately out to exploit you
- People with great intentions, yet maybe not fit for delivering on their guarantees

It will be significant that before you engage with anybody at any degree of business that you lead the proper degree of due diligence that incorporates performing foundation and reference checks. Keep in mind, the media ceaselessly helps us to remember the extortion that happens in business and you must do everything conceivable to abstain from becoming involved with it.

o Always have a leave technique - As a parallel to what they show you in protective driving courses, you ought to consistently backup investment, particularly if things begin to turn out badly. Successful leave procedures ought to be considered during the assessment and securing stages. For instance, how about we accept your investment technique was to buy a property with the goals of flipping it.

o Know your investment territory like a master - As an investor, it will be significant for you to have exhaustive information on your investment region. Despite the fact of having neighborhood experts to help you in finding, obtaining, and dealing with the properties is an extraordinary asset, you ought to never depend exclusively on them to figure out what a feasible investment opportunity is. Give yourself an opportunity to become more acquainted with your region and what an arrangement resembles. With this understanding, you will almost certainly go forward immediately, which is generally required on the best of the arrangements.

o Always assess the investment with property management charges included - Even on the off chance that you plan on dealing with the property yourself, it is astute to include the fitting property management expenses; this will cover you in the occasion you are never again ready to self-deal with the property.

o Have a decent comprehension of the four market cycles - Each market cycle accompanies diverse investment systems. When you become capable in distinguishing the market pointers, you will have more control on the most proficient method to deal with your portfolio and investment choices.

CHAPTER FIVE

HOW TO PROFIT FROM REAL ESTATE WITHOUT OWNING ANY PROPERTY

◆ ◆ ◆

Keen on benefitting from real estate? Searching for an option in contrast to contracts, dispossessions, occupants or flipping real estate? Acquiring the privilege to gather on reprobate real estate charges can be a worthwhile speculation even with restricted capital.

Regions generally evaluate charges on real estate to landowners every year and take into account an installment by a specific date. The bills are evaluated dependent on property estimation and can run from a couple of hundred dollars to a few thousand dollars. In the event that the they are not paid when due, they become degenerate. In numerous states, the provinces are permitted to dole out their entitlement to gather the wrongdoing to an investor.

At the point when the property owner pays the toll to the province, the investor gets their underlying venture.. On the off chance that a property owner neglects to pay within the required time allotted, the investor can start procedures to acquire a deed to the property. Assessment liens for the most part take over all other property obligations, including contracts.

Before making the venture, investigate the property to affirm it is attractive and to evade any property issues. Be sure the estimation of the property far surpasses the district duty bill. A general principle guideline is a property estimation multiple times the sum owed.

It is essential to understand the procedure and strategies will shift significantly by area and that not all states take an interest in expense lien deals. Additionally, remember there is a contrast between assessment lien authentications and duty deeds. Control and responsibility for property is just conceivable through a duty deed after any predefined recovery period has terminated.

For instance, in Orange County Florida, duties become reprobate for non-installment April 1 of the next year. The province at that point distributes the clearance of declarations in the paper during the long stretch of May.

An interested investor can enroll to offer on the endorsements at sale. Instead of a "face to face" sell off, the offering currently happens on the web. Bidders must save 10% of the sum they hope to go through with the district. Orange County can charge 18% on reprobate assessments so the offering begins at this greatest and is offered down. So a bidder willing to acquire 10% would prevail upon a bidder wanting 12%.

A triumphant bidder pays the area for the measure of reprobate duties and acquires their arrival when the bill is paid by the property owner (the province keeps the distinction in enthusiasm between the sum gathered and the financial specialists winning offer). Financial specialists owning endorsements that have not been paid or reclaimed by the landowner for a time of two years are qualified to apply for a duty deed deal. Most property landowners take care of their reprobate tab before it goes to the deed organize. This enables investors to acquire solid returns supported via real estate. At the point when a landowner neglects to pay, it is workable for a financial specialist to claim a property worth a lot of money for an investment of only a couple of hundred dollars with a lot bigger profits accessible for resale.

This present downturn of 2008 to 2010 has truly decimated the securities exchange which has constrained numerous individual financial specialists to reconsider their investment needs. A considerable lot of these financial specialists are beginning to search for elective types of contributing, one of which is real estate.

Presently, I know there's been a lodging market emergency that has reflected the financial exchange emergency from multiple points of view, however the reality continues as before that currently might be an ideal opportunity to get once again into real estate contributing. Costs have dropped significantly, now and then as much as 30 or 40% on properties no matter how you look at it in pretty much every area in America. That is my method for revealing to you that there are some staggering arrangements to be had right now which just vows to show signs of improvement over the long-term.

Today I need to discuss a couple of approaches to benefit from the current real estate contributing condition and give you a few things to concentrate on that you might not have thought of presently.

Today probably the best spot that we're seeing to put resources into real estate includes multi-family structures with up to 10 units. It's ideal to put resources into these multi-family structures in towns that you as of now live in. Try not to attempt to purchase a few of these in light of the fact that with our present economy, they may take more consideration and more acknowledgment on your part to get them up and profitable. This means owning one in the town you right now live to make things substantially simpler for you, in any event until further notice.

The incredible advantages of these kinds of investments are that they're little enough to be overseen by the landowner: you. One thing you're unquestionably going to need to investigate before you buy is present laws in regards to these sorts of structures.

Numerous towns have lease control laws just as non-ousting laws that make it significantly harder for you to dispose of occupants that aren't covering the tabs. Indeed, this might be the reason the present landowner has had so much issue that they need to sell. You can't make a profit if your occupants don't pay their lease and you can't oust them without burning through a lot of money in legitimate expenses and long periods of time.

Yet, if you can discover one of these investment properties in your general vicinity and there aren't any unfriendly laws that would influence you, presently may simply be the ideal time to swoop in and get it. Try not to be modest about offering absurdly low costs in light of the fact that numerous financial specialists are hoping to sell at any cost to get out from under their home loans.

Numerous investors obtained the properties with variable or movable rate home loans back when things were great and are presently finding that they can't renegotiate those advances on the grounds that the present condition of the economy and the financial market which are viably frigid credit for some individuals.

So there you have one straightforward approach to benefit in real estate, notwithstanding during a downturn.

With the current money related atmosphere the manner in which it is, investments are searching for financial specialists around the world. Financial exchanges are not working out quite as well, nor are the assets which contribute there. Gold has turned out to be too costly to even think about purchasing, as are numerous different assets. That doesn't leave investors numerous spots to get a decent return. With the exception of one kind of venture, the well-established ensured approach to get an arrival - real estate.

Customarily, real estate has been probably the most secure and long-term investment. There is constantly a requirement for lodging, and regardless of current money related markets, your venture is constantly protected and will quite often increment. Obviously, when we talk real estate investments, numerous individuals will think about the family home, however, there is more cash to be made in this industry.

The most well-known manner by which individuals profit in real estate is by buying the home or condo and renting it out to others for a charge every month.

Presently this might be to long-term tenants which are considered, more secure as the month to month rental expense is increasingly steady. Or on the other hand for lofts or homes in prevalent visitor goals, there is a rental charge for each night or week. This sort of occasion settlement will prompt much higher expenses, yet this may not be as steady, particularly on account of occasion goals with down occasions, (for example, winter in certain areas).

The two regular strategies where individuals pay for real estate investments are as per the following. For those with a lot of liquid money, they may possess the property completely. This recover from paying any interest and will mean any rental pay is coming directly into your pocket. Anyway for other people, who don't have the out and out capital or wish to possess many occasion homes, different bank and individual credits can be utilized to buy the property. With these advances one may pay the 'contract' during each time with the rental pay (as this will diminish the interest you pay)..

Regardless of how you choose to pay for real estate investments, be guaranteed they are an extraordinary cash creator and sure to bring on an arrival. If you take a look at a portion of the independent moguls around the globe, you will see something normal between almost every one of them. They profited in land ventures and property improvement. Frequently beginning with one property, these insightful financial specialists make such exceptional yields that they are before long controlling numerous properties and even their own high-rise structures. Start your adventure today and put resources into land to make a benefit.

Numerous individuals are thinking about venture realty to have something they could get cash from. It is tied in with making benefits that you also can get yourself into. Step into the real estate business world and produce proceeding with income with realty venture.

No degree or any instructive accomplishment is required to have realty for speculation. All you need is cash that will fill in as your capital and the correct information, which you can acquire even without taking care of a school. Appropriate learning on realty speculation can be gotten any place you are, even at home as long as you most likely are aware where to get supportive data or courses on the web.

As a potential realty financial specialist, it is basic for you to figure out how you can diminish all costs included and boost your income. You need to survey all that might be engaged with your endeavor like the rental rate, rental pay, property fix costs (current and future uses), profit that you can get in the event that you sell your property and quantifiable profit.

Starting in speculation realty isn't simple. Discovering venture realties can be so exceptionally testing however with the correct skill, appropriate instruction, key arranging and compelling techniques, you can clearly deal with and manage nearly everything without problems. If you are longing to proceed with stream of money with realty, try to stay up with the latest with the most recent patterns in realty venture and what can be normal later on.

Likewise, you need to discover yourself exactly how you can build up your net an incentive with a speculation realty that you can control. Other than purchasing a limited realty, there are numerous different things that you should consider other than low market worth cost. Numerous realty financial specialists are thinking about dispossessed homes that they can embellish and sell at a market worth cost.

In spite of the fact that dispossessed realties can be an achievable venture methodology, you must be cautious in deciding their good and bad times as now and again, these properties can just cost you more. A large number of these properties require costly fixes and exorbitant remodels. Being a financial specialist, you need to perform assessments either without anyone else or with an expert and get gauges for whatever expenses might be associated with improving the property.

You also need to make sense of when you can anticipate an arrival on speculation. If your picked realty will just motivate you to continue going through for a year as opposed to picking up inside three or four months, discover another venture realty and consider different methodologies that can give you incredible benefits.

You need an operator who has a decent notoriety and who acts rapidly for your benefit. For instance, will they demonstrate your property rapidly if a purchaser needs to see it? The operator who sold me the property I currently live in, wouldn't show it to me for 48 hours as he was too busy. When I advised the seller, she was angry with him. She was paying him all that commission and he wouldn't set aside the effort to show a purchaser round in an auspicious way. I don't know whether that specialist is still in business, however, there are some brilliant models that I can discuss having encountered them with the operator who sold me that house.

Most importantly, he was a liar. He advised the merchants that they needed to go out while he held an Open Home for imminent purchasers. I happened to drop by after the Open Home and I saw that no one had attended, yet he told the dealers that individuals came to the Open Home.

With this specific arrangement, I conflicted with my very own recommendation of never being the principal individual to name a cost. I was so amped up for the property, that I offered a significant expense at the start. After the arrangement was finished, the operator revealed to me that no one else would have offered such a significant expense for the property. I felt horrendous. Be that as it may, in a resulting exchange with the merchant, he made me feel somewhat better by saying from my point of view, I think you got a lot. From your point of view, you think you paid a lot for the property. Be that as it may, it was a great learning background. Try not to be the first to name a cost, do your exploration, yet even as the purchaser or the dealer, attempt to arrange a superior cost.

As the dealer, know that in the event that you have given the specialist time limits for him to be the sole operator before it goes on a numerous posting, they are regularly edgy to make a deal with the goal that they don't need to part their bonus. So regardless of whether they have done due industriousness, they are still prone to guide you to bring down your cost by 10% or 20% to get individuals keen on coming, and after that attempt to constrain you into selling route underneath the value you needed to acknowledge. Presently, when it goes on to various postings, in a decent economy your specialist probably won't put in a ton of exertion attempting to discover you a purchaser. In the downturn economy, they might be frantic enough to take the necessary steps to get you a purchaser, including utilizing harassing strategies to get you to bring down your asking cost. They don't stop for a second to utilize the dread factor. If you don't sell it at this value, you might clutch it for an extensive stretch of time. In the event that you do offer it at a much lower value, we'll have a greater amount of a chance to sell it for you.

A customer of mine was convinced to sell her home at closeout. She truly didn't know whether she needed to go that course, however the operator persuaded her that she could presumably go anyplace from $525K to $585K for her home - that it would be a speedy deal, she would get her cash, it would be finished. Spent over $5K on publicizing which the operator had coercively proposed, and after that the day preceding the property was to go to sell, the specialist called her and advised she expected to set her save cost at $450K and that she would be fortunate in the event that she even got that.

This is such gross absence of trustworthiness. They pull off this constantly. At no time when he was forcing her to put her property up at sale did he reveal to her that she would likely need to endure a shot of $130K. She accepted it with little or no evidence that she would leave the arrangement with a benefit. Rather, if he had his direction, he would have gotten the commission and she would have continued the misfortune. She came to me directly after the operator called her advising her to decrease her asking cost. She was in tears since she had just made an idea on another property, believing that she would have the cash from the closeout of this house. I prompted her not to proceed with the bartering. So, when she went in there that same night and disclosed to them she wasn't proceeding, they stated, "God help us, you can't do that." Also, she stated, "gracious yes I can, you're not getting my mark thus you can't sell my home."

Remember that specialists make their living from bonuses on deals. The commission depends on a level of the deal cost and is determined on a recipe the operator ought to unveil in many nations, in the event that you inquire. Like everything else in real estate it is debatable! Talk about the commission before making or accepting an offer.

The best time to deal over commission is the point at which the gatherings are near the point that it is just the commission that is standing out. Remember, operators are especially eager in the downturn market, and multiple times out of ten it fills in as they would very much want to sell a property and make some commission than let the deal fall through and make nothing by any means.

To summarize:

- guarantee that your operator will demonstrate your property in an auspicious way if a forthcoming purchaser turns up

- attempt to get suggestions for an operator who has uprightness and who is straightforward

- don't be pushed and don't get scared. It's your property, you're the one in control. Eventually, somebody will purchase your home.

CHAPTER SIX

HOW TO DETERMINE
A GOOD RENTAL PROPERTY

♦ ♦ ♦

Rental real estate is gradually turning into a wise investment attempt, despite the fact that there are some distrustful rare sorts of people who still believes that it's an overwhelming endeavor. Well we can't accuse them since scanning for a wise investment property is really hard. In any case, for those couple of positive thinkers, rental property is an incredible approach to aggregate riches.

Much the same as a business undertaking, it is significant that you have a solid arrangement or procedure on how you will build up your rental real estate into a lucrative undertaking. Else, you will wind up losing the majority of your investment. You have to do some meticulous research and most likely have a few associations with locate a gainful rental property. This is on the grounds that your goal is to make benefit inside the most limited time conceivable. This is additionally a similar motivation behind why you should discover a vender that is eager to give you free value.

Here are a few hints to enable you to begin with your rental real estate business:

1. You need an investment plan since this will enable you to decide the length of your ownership of specific rental property. Keep in mind that the more you claim the property, the more you'll spend on upkeep, fixes and upgrades. If you need to make any real enhancements for the property, make certain the deal cost will be sufficient to take care of the expense. In the event that you don't know, at that point better not spend excessively. In any case, owning the rental estate property for less time would likewise make greater investment hazard, particularly when purchasing in an overheated market. To make up for that hazard, you need a greater potential yearly return. For some little investors, be that as it may, long-term ownership is keen since it permits them a lot of time to outlive any vacillations in the market - and furthermore since the rental salary can be a decent beneficial pay meanwhile. Being a landowner is even a remunerating day work for a few.

2. There are different methods for discovering properties and these are as per the following: chase properties that

are now for abandonment, you will almost certainly get some data by methods for become a close acquaintance with city corridor assistants or bank workers who know about properties that are going to be dispossessed or are as of now abandoned; you may likewise attempt to contact a real estate operator who's vigilant for conceivable purchases; or you may join a neighborhood landowner or property owner's relationship with the goal for you to make contacts. And keeping in mind that you're grinding away, why not ask landowners straightforwardly to check whether they are ready to sell; you may take a stab at looking in papers for rental advertisements or you may drive around neighborhoods so as to scan "for lease" signs.

Get your funds fit as a fiddle

In the event that you really need to take part in a rental estate property business, you need a decent credit standing - which means less Visa obligation and other purchaser obligation. Lenders more often than not require greater up-front installments, charge higher loan costs and need your funds to be fit as a fiddle when you are purchasing rental properties.

It really pays to have a huge money hold in the wake of purchasing any property, since there may be some required fixes that rental property may require. In the event that you can bear to put aside in any event one month lease for every unit, which is a decent start. You may also attempt to apply for a credit extension, verified either by the property or your very own home so as to take care of bigger expenses.

Abstain from overspending

The motivation behind why you contribute on a rental estate property is for you to pick up benefits and not to lose each sparing you have. Ensure that despite everything, you have spared enough for your retirement before putting resources into rental real estate.Like any business wherein you will in general lose a few and afterward win some, attempt to spare as much as you could. Should be set up than be sorry later on.

Registration a Rental Property: Type of Property Desired

The main choice that you have to make is the sort of property that you need to put resources into. A great many people pick single family homes to begin since they are most acquainted with that sort of real estate. Condos, apartment suites, duplexes, and business property are for the most part reasonable sorts of rentals. Today, with the present condition of real estate, single-family homes are getting the most consideration. Numerous people are leasing instead of buying because of vulnerability in the economy. This has brought about rents being higher than ordinary; a circumstance that ought to be considered before purchasing rental property.

Locate a Real Estate Agent

Select a real estate specialist you can work with. Examine the sort of real estate you might want to put resources into and the value run. Disclose to the specialist that you will think about dispossessions and property that is recorded by the present owner. It is key that you set aside the effort to guarantee that the specialist comprehends that you are an investor and won't live in the property; your objective is full-time rental and income. The operator is roused by finding you a property to put resources into, which is the way he/she profits. You can anticipate that the real estate operator should disclose to you why the property will fit in with your craving to purchase a decent rental property.

Do Your Own Research

Research for the money saving advantages of the property ought to be finished by you. Decide the standard, interest, charges and home protection costs. This will require gauges for cost and loan cost that the real estate operator can assist you with. A traditionalist methodology is utilizing the approaching cost as the reason for cost. To decide rental value I like to add 30% to the entirety of these expenses to cover opening and fixes; utilize an assumption that is agreeable for you. Give this data to your real estate specialist; no sense in taking a look at properties where the asking cost is drives the rental cost out of thought. Find in any event three properties that fit your valuing criteria; this will enable you to move between the three properties during arrangement.

Arranging the deal

The exchange will be with an owner or on account of dispossessed property at the bank. Consulting with a mortgage holder is typically progressively troublesome because of the way that value development influences the owner legitimately. With a dispossession exchange, have the real estate specialist set up the gathering. The examination done above to decide rental cost will be comprehended and increased in value by an investor. If the bank is asking an excessive amount, it is anything but difficult to demonstrate that the property won't earn. Keep in mind, the bank has a non-performing resource that is costing cash for support, power, protection, and insurance from vandalism; they are roused to sell at a sensible cost.

Thought Questions for Purchasing a Rental Property

A landowner is just as fruitful as his property will enable him to be. In the event that you don't have a decent rental property or you overpaid for your property, you'll have a troublesome time discovering accomplishment as a landowner. Picking a rental property is the most significant choice you'll make, so you must be sure beyond a shadow of a doubt that you've placed in the examination to enable you to go to the correct choice.

When choosing a rental property, there are a few inquiries you have to consider.

- Can I bear the cost of the upfront installment? Numerous banks see rental property as a higher hazard, and accordingly, they frequently request a greater up-front installment on the credit. Here and there, they could request that you put down as much as 40% on the property. Converse with your bank to decide the amount you'll need to put down, and in the event that you can't realistically manage the cost of it, you'll have to think about another property to put resources into.

- Will the market rental worth spread the home loan? This comes down to basic arithmetic and Being a Landlord 101. Your rental rate needs to cover the home loan. In case you're paying more every month than you're acquiring, you're not going to make a benefit as a landowner (except if you're additionally living on the property). If the rental rate you need to cover the home loan isn't in accordance with the market esteem, you shouldn't make the investment.

- Is the structure appropriate for leasing? There are sure codes that structures need to meet before they can be leased lawfully. Acclimate yourself with the leasing laws in your general vicinity, and have the structure examined by an expert to make certain everything is up to code. If it's not up to code, you need to factor in the expenses of improving the structure to get it up to code. This is a significant advance, so ensure you don't skip it.

- Will any fixes or redesigns be made? Don't simply take a look at the sticker price on the property as it stands. You need to also consider any extra cash you'll have to place into the investment for updates. This could be anything from as little as changing the locks to as large as gutting the spot and remaking the internal parts. You need to consider each cost so you can decide whether it genuinely is a savvy investment.

- Is the property situated in a protected and secure zone? Wellbeing and security are constantly top worries for leaseholders, especially on the off chance that they have youngsters. If the property itself doesn't appear to be secure or it's in an especially hazardous neighborhood, you're most likely going to experience serious difficulties leasing it out and seeing an arrival on your investment. Look online for audits on neighborhood security, check wrongdoing insights, and take a drive around the region during the evening. Ensure there is a lot of lighting, and change/add locks to the entryways and windows.

Be endlessly careful when making an investment in rental property.

Step by step instructions to know a Good Rental Property

There are four principal factors that show whether a rental property is a decent bargain: the pay it creates, the area, the accessible financing and the honest estimation of the property with respect to the price tag. In this article, we will see how to investigate a rental property in one of these zones - assessing a properties salary - to know whether you are really getting a lot.

Stage One: Analyzing Cash Flow

- Cash Flow Analysis: After acquiring some basic data from the dealer, you can sort out and dissect that data to decide the measure of positive or negative income an imminent property will deliver. Try to utilize yearly numbers as opposed to monthly when finishing your income investigation. Give us a chance to survey the Property Cash Flow Analysis:

- Gross Income: In this area of the Cash Flow Analysis, an investor includes the planned or anticipated rents and all other anticipated that salary should decide the Gross Scheduled Income (GSI). He then subtracts the opportunity stipend or anticipated opening, taken from the present opportunity rate for the zone, to land at the Gross Effective Income (GEI).

- Expenses: Here, the investor decides the all-out Operating Expenses (OE) by including every one of the costs engaged with the activity of the property excluding any obligation administration.

- Net Operating Income: The Net Operating Income (NOI) is the contrast between the Gross Effective Income and the Operating Expenses

- Debt Service: Debt Service (DS) is the complete head and interest installments for every one of the home loans or credits used to secure the property.

- Cash Flow: The property's Cash Flow or Net Income (NI) is the Net Operating Income less the complete Debt Service (DS). This can be a positive or negative number.

Stage Two: Verifying the Numbers

In some cases, to get a higher price tag, a vender will blow up the measure of salary a property produces or basically neglect to specify the majority of the costs really required to keep up the property. Regularly, the vender will be totally fair with the data he supplies, yet some significant makes sense of are accidentally left. For instance, this could occur if the merchant deals with the property himself and does exclude a property management expense in the numbers he gives you. The merchant might not have stayed aware of essential fixes and upkeep on the property, in which case the costs he supplies may not be adequate for you to sufficiently keep up the property. Shockingly, if the purchaser puts together his idea with respect to wrong data, he could lose a great deal of cash. As the purchaser, you should shield yourself from this by confirming the majority of the data you get on a property. You should take the data you get from the dealer carefully until you have confirmed its exactness. There are various approaches to check a property's salary and costs:

- Property Operating Statements: These announcements are regularly alluded to as Profit and Loss or Income and Expense proclamations. A decent investor will track all the pay and costs delivered by his property on a month to month and yearly premise. You can look at the data furnished by these announcements with the data that the dealer at first gave. It is a smart thought to get the property's Operating Statements for the previous three entire years just as year-to-date. Be careful about adulterated data. Numerous merchants and realtors will dishonestly publicize a property's Operating Statements by furnishing a planned purchaser with a Pro-forma. A Pro-forma does not take its numbers from what the property really created, yet rather gives their gauge of what the property should deliver. The overall gain appeared by these assessments are quite often definitely higher than what the property is really creating. The vender or realtor will endeavor to legitimize the evaluated numbers over the genuine numbers by proposing that the present rents are low, or if some minor fixes are done the property's estimation would increment. Regardless of what their reasons are, your offer ought to be received from the numbers that the property is right now creating. In the event that you can build its incentive through lease expands, fixes or whatever it might be, the advantage ought to be yours, not the seller's.

- Schedule E(s): A Schedule E is the government tax document that reports real estate pay and costs. The property's addition or misfortune as appeared on this structure is then added to the owner's other salary to decide his government annual assessment commitment. Timetable Es will give the most exact bookkeeping of a property's salary and costs. This is in such a case that the merchant has forgotten about costs that he has paid on his property; at that point, his assessment commitment will be higher. Since nobody needs to make good on additional in regulatory obligations, they remember to incorporate any of the appropriate costs. A merchant may admit that he included a bigger number of costs or recorded less pay than there really was so as to bring down his duty commitment. Regardless of what is asserted, you need just pass by what is set up on the Schedule E. In the event that the dealer lied on his government forms, a lower price tag for his property might be the outcome. Try not to go out on a limb by going on somebody's promise alone.

There are costs that are at times excluded on the Schedule E that you should include when investigating a property's pay: property management, yard support, and snow evacuation. There are additionally a few costs on the Schedule E that you can prohibit: devaluation, interest, dinners and diversion, and travel. In looking into the Schedule Es, demand duplicates of at any rate the previous three years. Be careful with exceptional decreases in rental salary over these years. This could demonstrate a negative change in the market or the region's economy. If there is such a decay, attempt to decide its motivation so you can all the more astutely continue with or end the investigation procedure.

Not all investors utilize a 1040 Form Schedule E to report their real estate salary. On the off chance that they claim their property in an organization, at that point they won't utilize this structure. If so, despite everything, you need to investigate a similar data that would be accounted for on a Schedule E. You can do this by mentioning from the dealer duplicates of all government forms identifying with the property and social event the data from them.

- Utility Companies: By calling the service organizations, you can discover the property's careful utility cost history.

- County Tax Assessor's Office: The assessor's office has record all property charge commitments, just as any unpaid property charges.

- Lease Agreements: By looking into the present leases, you will know the careful measure of lease that the property right now creates.

- Market Rents: However a property might be as of now getting a specific sum in rents, it is as yet conceivable that these rents are not true. If a property is leased anomalous higher than the equitable rates, another purchaser will battle to get them leased for a similar sum when the present leases lapse. Acclimate yourself with current market leases so you can make the suitable changes in accordance with your offer.

- Insurance Company: Insurance rates will fluctuate from customer to customer and friends to organization. Along these lines, you can't expect that your protection rate for a property will be actually equivalent to the current owner's; nonetheless, they are normally genuinely close. Call around and check rates from various organizations to locate the best one for you. Make a point to think about comparable plans. In the event that the inclusion being offered isn't the equivalent, at that point the rates will be extraordinary. You have to analyze rates for a similar inclusion. Ensure that the organization you pick has aggressive rates, but on the other hand is an outstanding, legitimate organization.

The most effective method to Determine If a Multifamily Property Is a Good Investment

There are a few different ways that you measure how fruitful a particular multifamily property investment is probably going to be. You could take a look at the rental development rates and the opening inhabitance rates to decide how well a specific rental property is doing at present, yet these numbers won't demonstrate to you how well this particular property will perform later on. You could likewise decide to just buy multifamily real estate properties in the beach front markets, or the business sectors that are as of now creating a great deal of ROI. This, nonetheless, will make them contend with each other investor in the nation for properties that may not be worth what you will pay for them or fundamentally produce long-term gains later on. You would prefer not to just see things like inhabitance rates, rental development rates or how appealing the area of the property is on the off chance that you need to precisely check the investment estimation of the property. To really decide whether a specific multifamily investment property merits your time, take a look at the best 4 parts of a top business rental investment. In fifth spot underneath, some last tips before you pull the trigger on your new investment.

1. Great Population Growth

The best places to find great multifamily investment properties are areas that show exceptionally solid developments in populace. There are not many things that produce enthusiasm for rental properties like a detonating populace. Areas that have a critical inundation of new inhabitants are the best places to purchase business real estate. The explanation for an area's populace blast is an interesting point in any case. The best areas are ones that are picking up populace through relocation or the formation of new families. Spots where new individuals are joining existing families are not as valuable to the business property investor.

2. Occupants Who Are Young and Mobile

Areas with more noteworthy quantities of youthful and versatile occupants are better for rental property owners, as more youthful individuals will in general lease homes more than they get them.

3. Areas with Expanding Employers

At the point when a huge organization extends its business base, increasingly youthful and versatile tenants move into that area. This makes the business rental properties around there progressively significant to investors. Savvy investors put their cash into business sectors that show solid rising patterns in bosses and employment development. Search for areas with better than expected development in work or areas where enormous businesses are opening for business. Chances are, these huge organizations will acquire a ton of new inhabitants, who will all need a loft to lease.

4. Explicit Submarkets

Most business lodging investors search for business sectors that are either delegated high obstruction, implying that it is hard to locate a rental loft for the leaseholder (think New York City) or markets that are anything but difficult to locate a rental property (like Texas). If you set aside the effort to locate a quite certain submarket in a simple to get into territory, you could discover the big stake for business real estate here. For instance, most pieces of Texas are anything but difficult to locate a rental condo, with the exception of a not many areas that are viewed as recently grew top of the line markets. These high boundary areas in simple market territories make great real estate investments.

5. Property by Property Analysis

When you have limited your investment down to explicit submarkets you have to weigh out various investment properties inside that region. Here a specialist with involvement in property management and ownership is your most solid option for finding incredible multifamily investment properties. Try not to think the leaflets you get from operators contain anything besides the rosiest forecasts. Get somebody who can really endorse your investment for what it will do or as near it as could be expected under the circumstances. This isn't only a scientific endeavor dependent on salary, expressed costs, obligation administration, and different expenses. You need somebody to do the majority of this inside the structure of cautious property due steadiness and information of market points of interest where property management is concerned. You need somebody who will factor in your important capital enhancements, cautiously survey occupant data, and different issues that may come up during a property examination. Two "indistinguishable" structures beside one another on a similar road may perform diversely relying upon how they have been overseen before, the inhabitant base, owner relations with neighbors and nearby experts, etc. The factors are many. Ensure you get the most experienced financier and property management individual you can to speak to you.

CHAPTER SEVEN

HOW TO DETERMINE WHAT TYPE OF RENTAL TO BUY

◆ ◆ ◆

Rental properties can be amazingly gainful in any economy. The focal points ought to be self-evident. To give some examples, month to month income, incentive for a long-term investment, and with the vulnerability of the economy and individuals losing their home to abandonments, numerous new properties are available at a diminished rate and a lot more individuals are going to leasing as the main alternative.

When you are thinking about rentals as a possibility for your portfolio, presently is a perfect time to do as such. Outfitted with the correct learning of how to prevail with rentals, you can to benefit from the current monetary condition. Actually you can do so fiercely and getting to be well off all the while. Envision repeating month to month salary from stable long-term occupants.

What is required is the eagerness to go out on a limb associated with acquiring any property for a rental. Obviously, it must be an educated and it must be vital as far as area and where you will locate the most ideal leaseholders and where your property estimation will increment. This may take some time and exertion to investigate, however, there are numerous open doors where a key money related choice including great sound judgment can be made.

Numerous individuals are hesitant to purchase any properties right now because of all the dread and vulnerability encompassing our economy. Others are looking for the open door that exists because of the new conditions that have surfaced in light of the lodging business sector breakdown. In the event that you are one of the ones who are frightful or dubious, the best counsel I could offer is to look carefully and in detail at the upsides of rental properties.

When you have concluded that you need to profit by the income of rental properties, there are three explicit ways that you can make your properties incredibly beneficial.

1.) Quality management: The more you can think about the properties and put resources into their upkeep, with both the present moment and long-term at the top of the priority list, the more beneficial they will turn into. A few owners concede upkeep to not far off and shockingly, it thinks about the nature of the management and the long-term estimation of the property.

2.) Location and Quality of Tenants: Depending on where the rental property is found will decide the nature of leaseholders and the value that can be charged per tenant. Clearly the objective is to have long-term tenants paying a premium for a quality rental. This will augment your arrival on investment and increment your income month to month.

3.) Attention to Tenant Retention: To keep your occupants, they basically should be seen as your benefits and along these lines treating them and their needs and demands with the most astounding need. Numerous property owners disregard their tenants and don't serve them or their needs. This will just prompt high opportunity rates which will affect your month to month income among different issues.

You can augment your pay and monthly income through rental properties with practically zero cerebral pain. Right now is an ideal opportunity to start to learn, research and start the way toward doing the math so as to settle on educated choices about the most ideal areas and properties to gain.

Instructions to Buy Investment Rental Property

With the cost of houses dropping, you might consider how to purchase investment rental property as a benefit making system. The objective is to discover reasonable real estate that you can rapidly lease to occupants. The contrast between what you pay on home loan and upkeep and what the rental pay ought to be a decent positive income.

Putting resources into rental property delivers practically easy revenue, which implies that once everything is set up, the benefits come in predictably on a month to month premise. Sometimes there will be time and additional cash required in the upkeep of the property. Due determination in exploring the property and the state of house will give you a smart thought of what fixes should be made en route.

I feel compelled to pressure this progression as much as possible. Ensure you set aside the effort to get the property assessed to maintain a strategic distance from huge forthright support charges. Check whether the property as of now has a rental history and get some information about the exhibition of rentals in the territory you are looking.

In the event that you are new to putting resources into rental property, there is a decent possibility you don't really realize where to start. Here are a couple of pointers to begin:

- Figure out your investment spending plan and how you will fund the upfront installment. This is an entire article in itself, however I can reveal to you that banks are searching for a 20% up front installment

- Do some examination on fixed rate and variable rate contracts

- Get your home loan agent to prequalify you for the buy

- Decide on the area where you need to possess rental properties

- Contact a nearby realtor's office and converse with a realtor who has some expertise in the purchasing and selling of investment properties

- Join a system of different people who are specialists at putting resources into real estate. They can enable you to decide a decent area to purchase rental properties and answer some other inquiries you may have. There are a few decent online informal organizations for real estate investors also.

Putting resources into real estate can give you a feasible wellspring of positive salary if you are eager to place in the exploration required to settle on a wise investment choice. You can discover progressively about how to purchase investment rental property that is in a top-notch area for tenants by asking at your nearby realtor's office or joining a system of different investors.

Properties of Rental Investment: Time to Buy or Sell

How can one decide when to sell a rental property investment? If you are going to purchase rental properties, having an arrangement set up for the fitting time to sell is significant.

I have worked with numerous people throughout the years and told them the best way to purchase rental property. There are numerous things that should be viewed as when acquiring for investment purposes. There is additionally - certainly - an opportunity to sell.

Step by step instructions to Buy an Investment Property

- Is the property in a helpful area? Is it close to shopping, in an area with great schools, and is it effectively available to interstates and associating streets?

- Does the potential investment property have a sound establishment? What kind of issues does the home have? In the event that it needs another rooftop or the establishment is depressed in and is making issues inside the structure, it probably won't be a wise investment right now. In the event that the issues are just corrective, such as another washroom floor, painting or covering, it might be advantageous. Examination reports will uncover the property's defects so the purchaser and real estate expert can settle on a decent choice.

- Do you have a sufficient up-front installment to buy the rental property so financing won't be an issue? In the present real estate showcase, most loan specialists will see an upfront installment of 40-half as a decent hazard. In the event that you can put 100% into the property - this is shockingly better.

- Income picked up from the property needs to surpass costs. Distinguish a credit commendable occupant, a dependable property director, and a strong rent to make your property investment gainful. Property management expenses are charge deductible.

- For private property investments, single-family homes just as multi-inhabitant properties, for example, duplexes and fourplexes are incredible approaches to manufacture pay and riches. A few investors might need to consider high rises. For this situation, a business property advance will be important to get financing.

- Use devaluation on the investment property as an approach to get a yearly finding charge. Check with your bookkeeper, who will apply the deterioration finding on the structure, apparatuses - even window medications. The administration still permits charge conclusions for quickened devaluation on properties. Sharp real estate investors utilize this conclusion to build income and net working benefit on a property.

At the point when to sell a Rental Property

I have a term for properties that should be sold: gator properties. These are properties that are eating the investor buzzing with conveying costs. At the point when an investor takes a look at the main concern on a croc property - there is no benefit - just costs. A croc property today may have been a wise investment ten years back. However, a few people will keep on holding a property until it drains the majority of the benefits they may have made in the initial 5-7 years.

If a property has nostalgic worth (it was your first home), a few investors may will in general need to clutch it. Having an enthusiastic connection to an investment property that should create salary isn't great. Some of the time an individual will hold this sort of property regardless of whether it isn't productive. It might be a great opportunity to think about selling this property.

- After a specific number of years, the deterioration charge finding is spent on a property. Ask your bookkeeper when this deterioration is never again relevant. At the point when the investment can never again be deteriorated, it's an ideal opportunity to sell that property and buy another rental.

- Consider selling the property and applying the 1031 duty code, so no capital additions assessment is forced on the benefits. To summarize, the code expresses that an owner can sell one property in return for a securitized bit of property or occupant in like manner bit of property. Fold the benefits from one property into another investment to build riches and look after it.

- Generally, in the twelfth year of property ownership - the time has come to sell an investment. The choice to sell will rely upon two elements.

1. Is there enough value in the property to sell? Or then again, have you hauled out an excessive amount of value in the property?

2. Will the real estate market enable you to sell and get a decent benefit? Approach a real estate proficient for a custom market examination on the property to check whether it's realistic to get a value that nets a pleasant benefit.

- Alligator properties are not productive for an assortment of reasons. I am astounded at the quantity of investors who are not in any case mindful that their property is losing cash. In the event that you have a property that may lose cash, at that point, ask your real estate expert or bookkeeper to play out an expense to pay investigation. On the off chance that it is in fact a crocodile property - think about selling.

Investors purchase and sell values constantly. There is an opportunity to buy and an opportunity to sell a home too.

Ten Buying Tips for Rental Properties

Purchasing rental properties is a decent method to build your advantages. Be that as it may, picking the correct rental property will challenge. Here are a couple of things to check for preceding purchasing rental property.

1. Area - Most individuals would prefer not to live in the shelter docks. The area of your rental property will decide how simple it will be to lease. In the event that you have a ton of vehicle traffic, you may get a more noteworthy reaction from a sign at the area than you will from a paper include.

Occupants need to live in pleasant neighborhoods near every one of the comforts. They need to be near the schools, stores, recreational areas, medical clinics, and work. I haven't met any individual who needs to live in a bothersome neighborhood or drive 15 minutes for a gallon of milk.

2. Numbers - When purchasing rental property you need to check the numbers. Ensure you have every one of the costs related with that property and ensure despite everything it has a positive income. Contemplate the upkeep issues, any utilities not secured by inhabitant and

amortize the expense of the huge activities like heater substitution, new material, siding or finishing.

These tasks just happen once every 15-20 years however you might come in to this in the tenth year of that cycle. Make sure to compute your costs high and your salary low. This can spare you a few astonishments not far off. Anticipate that the unit should be vacant in a month out of every year because of turnover. You should repaint and clean the rugs in the initial 2 weeks; at that point, promote and demonstrate the following 2 weeks. You should just rely on 11 months of lease for every year.

3. Lower Maintenance Buildings - You need to keep away from homes that will require costly routine support. A few models would be homes that have cedar-shake shingles or siding, wood sided structures, wood outline windows, block garages, cedar decks, and so forth.

Attempt to look not far off and decide the future support needs. Keep in mind the lower the upkeep the less migraines and bigger benefits.

4. Higher Home Prices - Check in towns with higher home costs, since this expands the interest for rental property. Search for the monstrous house on the square that has a lower cost, empowering you to buy inside the edges.

After some inside and outside paint, somewhat light finishing and new drapes, viola', a house that will get premium lease as a result of the class of neighborhood. On the off chance that individuals can't stand to purchase a home in this class they should lease. This will make an interest for rental property.

5. Beneath Market Rent costs - When purchasing rental property, search for rental property which has lease costs that are underneath ebb and flow market rents. This will enable you to raise the lease and increment the estimation of the property. According to over, this may simply require a little cushion to empower raising the rental cost.

Rental property market worth is controlled by the measure of pay gotten by the rental property. Remember, if the rental property has leaseholders when you buy it, they dislike it when you raise the lease. Additionally, verify what kind of rent is set up. The rent goes with the deal. In the event that the present tenant is paying an unsatisfactory cost and has 1/2 a year left on the rent it could end up being a losing recommendation.

There is just a single method to stop a rent as another owner. You should redesign the spot. Check with the nearby lodging commission to perceive what the base cost prerequisites of redesigning are for quick expulsion of current rent holders.

6. Great Rental History - Whenever purchasing rental properties, you should check the rental history. Verify overall to what extent tenants are staying and do they pay their lease on schedule. A few neighborhoods are normally snappy turnover times. Close to air terminals, uproarious bars or clubs, close to army installations, and so forth.

7. Agrees to Zoning and Fire Codes - Make sure you verify whether there are reviews required by nearby authorities for rental properties and does this property pass those assessments. You never know the real reason the present owner is selling the property.

It might require broad fixes to pass the investigations. A brisk warning would be if the power has been off for more than 90 days. They will as a rule require a review before reestablishing power, particularly in the event that it is a known rental.

8. Under Twenty Years Old - This is clear as crystal, in the event that you confine your choice to structures that are under twenty years of age, you will constrain the odds that the structure will have any construction regulation or upkeep issues. The structure could be close to the upkeep cycle for rooftop, paint and potentially heater yet the structure will be sound and not requiring redesigned windows, siding or concrete fix.

9. Out of State Owners or Managers - When purchasing rental property, search for properties that are claimed by out of state owners. It is difficult to oversee rental property from out of state and when these come available to be purchased, the owners are normally more worried about selling rapidly than getting as much as possible.

So as to lease a spot rapidly, you should live close by so you can demonstrate it at the guest's solicitation. As a rule, they will request to see it in the following 20 minutes or thereabouts. Take into account their solicitations and show it snappy. Most tenants need a spot inside the following week or something like that and won't hold on to see your place until one week from now since you are occupied.

Most occasions they will settle on a choice before tomorrow when it would be progressively advantageous for you to indicate it. This has transpired too ordinarily. Never give out the location for drive-by. Forthcoming leaseholders will request the location to do a drive by and simply take a look at the spot. Try not to burn through your time with these people. Demand demonstrating it in the following 30 minutes or you won't give out the location as a graciousness to the neighbors.

10. Neighborhood is steady or improving - clearly maintain a strategic distance from neighborhoods that are declining, take a look at the composition on the

dividers and remain out. In spite of the fact that these may look great because of the low-price tag, they are hard to gather the rents.

By discovering neighborhoods that are steady or improving, it will be simpler to lease the property and you will almost certainly expand the lease. The general accord is, the better the area, the higher the price tag and the higher the lease costs, in this way the edge for benefit is more noteworthy. The less fortunate the area the lower the price tag and lower the lease costs decreasing the overall revenues.

CHAPTER EIGHT

HOW TO FIND LOW COST PROPERTIES

♦ ♦ ♦

What is the best alternative for your money investment? Generally safe investments that give an exceptional yield on investment, obviously! That is the reason such a significant number of effective investors go to real estate putting resources into rental properties.

Be that as it may, shouldn't something be said about the majority of the stories you've caught wind of real estate investors losing huge amounts of cash from rental properties? They're most likely racing into your brain as you hear "Purchasing rental property is perhaps the best choice for okay investments."

The reason these accounts exist. Each choice a real estate investor makes when purchasing rental property influences whether it will be an okay money investment or not. In this way, if a real estate investor does not adapt precisely how to discover generally safe investments when purchasing rental property, his/her real estate investment can come up short.

In any case, rental properties can be the best generally safe investments.

For what reason are rental properties the best Low Risk Investments?

Before figuring out how to discover okay investments when purchasing rental property, realize you're settling on the correct decision for your money investment. Investigate why rental properties are the best generally safe investments.

Investment Properties Generate Monthly Rental Income

When purchasing rental property is done well, a real estate investor can begin making positive income from rental salary inside the main month or something like that. No other generally safe investments enable the investor to begin making cash back on a money investment so rapidly without selling.

Investment Properties Are Tangible Income Producing Assets

The watchword here is "substantial". In the wake of purchasing rental property and checking the accomplishment through positive money flow (or scarcity in that department), a real estate investor can make a move and influence change. Having the option to control the accomplishment of a money investment makes rental properties generally safe investments.

Investment Properties Appreciate in Value

Other than profiting from rental pay, the estimation of investment properties will in general go up. Particularly in the present lodging market, which is a seasonally tight advertise all around, gratefulness will in general occur at a quicker rate. This implies selling these okay investments quite often ensures an exceptional yield on investment.

Steps to Finding Low Risk Investments When Buying Rental Property

We presently realize that rental properties can be generally safe investments, yet there are sure stages a real estate investor can take to guarantee he/she finds an okay real estate investment.

Step #1: Location in the Real Estate Market

The initial step is pinpointing the best places to put resources into real estate for generally safe investments. An area in the real estate market can influence everything about okay investments: their capacity to pull in inhabitants, cause rental salary, to create positive income, and sell for a decent rate of return. There are two sections to this progression when purchasing rental property: picking a city with a promising real estate market and finding the best neighborhood for investment properties.

The Ideal Real Estate Market for Low Risk Investments

A real estate showcase with the best places to put resources into real estate will above all else have a sound economy that displays work development. Search for a real estate advert that has new rising organizations or effective organizations that are growing or moving to the city. This will prompt populace development and an expanding interest for investment properties.

A real estate investor should investigate the unemployment rate of an area just as the enhancement of the business. An area subject to one industry could mean awful things for real estate contributing if that industry falls or migrates.

The real estate showcase you pick when purchasing rental property can really represent the deciding moment the arrival on investment. Search at an area with minimal effort to lease proportion for the best okay investments. A decent degree of profitability comes when a real estate investor can charge a decent lease value contrasted with the price tag of the investment property.

The Ideal Neighborhood for Low Risk Investments

Picking the best places to put resources into real estate doesn't stop at finding an incredible real estate advertise. The decision of neighborhood for investment properties is similarly as significant, as the real estate contributing potential can differ from neighborhood to neighborhood. In the event that you need a simple method for picking the best places to put resources into real estate, investigate the area to guarantee it advantageously has walkability and access to open transportation, low wrongdoing rates, and great school locale to guarantee investment properties will be generally safe in that area.

Step #2: The Condition of Investment Properties

When a real estate investor has discovered the absolute best places to put resources into real estate, it's an ideal opportunity to pick a genuine investment property. Perform investment property examination to choose which investment property will be a standout amongst other generally safe investments.

Investment property examination will help a real estate investor decide whether the state of the rental property will help in getting a decent rate of profitability or hurt its odds. The best generally safe investments in real estate don't require an excessive number of fixes, yet still, have some space for constrained appreciation. An investment property with restorative fixes like a requirement for new paint, covering, or another apparatus or two is a sheltered decision for your money investment.

A home review ought to uncover what fixes are required. Investment properties with major auxiliary issues, rooftop harm or water and electrical framework harm won't make for okay investments.

Investment property investigation, just as home review, ought to uncover the age of the investment property, which a real estate investor needs to contemplate when purchasing rental property. Why? The more established the investment property, the more upkeep and fixes it will require. Regardless of whether the home investigation uncovers no requirement for fixes now, an old investment property will require them soon, later on. Here is the manner by which to think about the ages of an investment property and the fixes required:

• 5-10 years of age: practically no upkeep

• 10-20 years of age: more upkeep

• 20-30 years of age: will require substantially more fix: rooftop, water warmer, funneling, and so forth.

Make certain to check the home review report; more seasoned rental properties that have had a profound redesign as of late can at present be generally safe investments.

Step #3: Return on Investment

A system that guarantees general safety of investments is real estate contributing for positive income. On the off chance that a real estate investment has positive income from the beginning, a real estate investor will profit when an inhabitant is set up to give rental pay.

Positive income is the point at which the yearly rental pay of an investment property surpasses the majority of the costs required to claim and look after it (fixes, charges contract, and so forth.). Proceeding with investment property examination, a real estate investor must complete computations to decide whether there will be sure income for an exceptional yield on investment.

The best rate of profitability metric to use for investment property investigation is money on money return:

Money on Cash Return = (Cash Flow/Cash Invested) x 100

With a positive income, the money on money return estimation will demonstrate a positive rate of profitability. Real estate specialists concur that any investment property which can give 8% or higher will expedite a decent return investment and positive income.

Step #4: Exit Strategy

The last advance in discovering generally safe investments in the real estate market is ensuring a leave technique is set up before purchasing rental property. There are two principle leave procedures in real estate contributing:

- Buy and hold (long-term or present moment)

- Selling the investment property

Either leave methodologies ought to apply to generally safe investments effectively: one as the leave procedure to utilize quickly and the different as a reinforcement leave system, on the off chance that things don't go as arranged.

Rental properties can be generally safe investments for profiting in real estate. A real estate investor simply needs to make the correct strides when purchasing a rental property. Concentrate on the area, the state of the investment property, and the arrival on investment, and plan for a leave technique.

Great Rental Property Choosing Tactics

What would be a good idea for me to search for in an investment property? This is a typical inquiry for real estate investors. Figuring out how to decide a decent rental property will mean the distinction between a gainful investment and a terrible investment.

There are various elements that go into deciding whether a rental property is a wise investment. This article will disclose when to purchase dependent on market cycles, where to purchase, what kind of investment property to purchase, and what a decent return on an investment property is.

At the point when to Buy Rental Property

Understanding business sector cycles will enable you to choose when to purchase. To do this, you should almost certainly perceive if the zone you're taking a look at is an economically tight advertise or a wide-open market.

As we are hoping to purchase an extraordinary rental property, we need to purchase during a fast-moving business sector. A fast-moving business sector is when there are numerous homes available and not a ton of purchaser's – giving purchaser's everything the power. Purchase during a fast-moving business sector. Sell during an economically tight showcase.

Where to Buy Rental Property

Much the same as the climate, real estate is very area subordinate. The real estate market can be hot in one town and cold in the following. Indeed, even inside a similar city, you can have more than one real estate showcase. The area of a property is commonly viewed as the absolute most significant factor in deciding its worth.

You need to search for a property in a decent neighborhood, in a decent school area, near employments and nearby pleasantries. These components will probably build the estimation of your rental after some time – as long as these variables remain the equivalent.

The most effective method to Spot Good Locations

There are incredible markets everywhere throughout the nation. In each state, you can discover pockets of business sectors on the precarious edge of development. Here is a portion of the criteria we search for:

• Is it situated close to a major city? Enormous urban communities can extend employment opportunity expansion, alongside culture, nightlife and helpful comforts.

• How enormous is the populace and is it developing? Hope to put resources into urban communities with more than 1 million occupants. In many zones, around 40% of the populace rents, which leaves 400,000 potential occupants for your rental property.

• You don't need to purchase a property in a major city. The key is to take a look at a whole metro zone to decide the best neighborhoods. You may find that there is really a more noteworthy interest to purchase in the suburbs of a major city, where the rates are lower, schools are better and the enhancements are more pleasant. Try not to purchase excessively far away from the city as individuals for the most part would prefer not to live over 30 minutes away.

• Is it decent to advertise? Investors can decide whether the territory is encountering a purchaser's or economically tight showcase by checking stock levels and to what extent it takes for a property to sell (normal number of days on market, or DOM).

• Are home costs expanding or diminishing every month? A decent general guideline is to see home estimation drifts over a continuous multi month time span.

• Is there rental interest? Sites and neighborhood property supervisors can give data about rental interest in the region.

• Does the zone have a low middle or normal home cost? Middle home costs are essentially the widely appealing properties. In a moderate market, the normal home cost ought to be close to 3 to multiple times the normal pay.

What Type of Rental Property Should I Buy?

There are various approaches to profit in real estate. You may put resources into a business property, mechanical property, a whole high rise or a solitary family home.

Whatever you choose is the best course for you, pick one, gain proficiency with the intricate details, stick to it and become a specialist. You can't do everything, in the event that you need to do it well. Pick the system that works for you and put your vitality into that by itself.

The single-family home is the least difficult approach to begin as another real estate investor. Furthermore, numerous master investors will reveal to you it's the absolute best investment in real estate. From our experience, the best kind of single-family homes have in any event 3 rooms and 2 showers.

When you consider what you search for in a home for your family, odds are it's a solitary family home and not a duplex, triplex, townhouse or condo. Single-family homes are much simpler to both lease and sell than multi-family homes.

In the event that you are attempting to sell a multi-unit property, no doubt different investors will hope to get it. As we understand, investors are continually searching for an arrangement and would prefer not to pay the maximum. While single-family homes can be offered to people in general at retail cost. If your property is reasonable to the normal purchaser, you ought to hope to have a lot of interest when you sell or lease.

This is particularly obvious when you've set aside the effort to purchase a decent rental property. Where it's situated in a decent neighborhood, with great schools, near occupations and access to nearby luxuries.

More reasons we like to put resources into single-family homes:

- Easier to upkeep

- Higher quality tenants

- Faster appreciation

- Easier Financing

- Affordable value focuses

Instructions to Analyze Investment Properties

When you're out taking a look at potential investment properties, it's essential to realize how to break them down. Accepting you've pursued our tips on where to get, you at that point need to run the numbers. This incorporates the anticipated lease and every one of the expenses or costs related. Remember to incorporate closing costs, escrow expenses, potential opportunity and home loan expenses.

While there might be a great deal of costs, make sure to consider month to month lease, energy about the property, yearly increment in lease and tax cuts you fit the bill for. Each and every time you take a look at a home, make a point to utilize your income investigation condition and let the numbers represent themselves.

After you've separated every one of the numbers, you would then be able to choose if this rental is going to accommodate your investment procedure and produce positive income. In case you're uncertain how to figure income returns on a property, visit our site to download a free income investigation spreadsheet.

To recap, here's the manner by which to decide a decent rental property:

• Located in an alluring territory close to occupations

• Ideally in a metro zone with more than 1 million individuals

• Single-family homes

• Well-kept up and refreshed

• Priced in the middle range for the zone

• Priced between $100,000 to $200,000

What is a Good Return on Investment Property?

Contingent upon who you ask, anything over a 15% ROI could be viewed as a decent return on a real estate investment. Be that as it may, there are a couple of approaches to precisely ascertain your potential rate of return.

Ascertaining ROI

The return on investment (ROI) is a measure used to assess the proficiency or benefit of an investment. As it were, the measure of return with respect to the investment's expense.

Return on initial capital investment = Annual rental salary/Total money investment

Computing Capitalization Rate

The capitalization rate or top rate is the pace of profit for a salary property dependent on the net operating income (NOI). The top rate demonstrates the pace of return considering your strategy for financing. Investors for the most part consider a decent top rate above 8%, and particularly 10%.

Top rate = NOI/Price

Computing Cash on Cash Return

A money on money return or COC return, measures the yearly return on your investment dependent on the NOI and the all-out money investment. Your COC changes relying upon various financing techniques. Generally, a great COC return is above 8%, yet go for above 10% or 12%.

COC Return = NOI/Total money investment

In contrast to the financial exchange, real estate is simpler to foresee, on the if you realize what to search for. To remain over market cycles in the zone your rental is found, you have to focus on any changes.

Essentially go on the web and search for school evaluations, nearby bosses, wrongdoing rates, rental rates, home rates and populace shifts. In the event that you notice negative things occurring around there, you can generally choose to offer your rental property before qualities start to diminish and purchase in a best in class neighborhood.

CHAPTER NINE

HOW TO SET THE RIGHT PRICE FOR YOUR REAL ESTATE LISTING

◆ ◆ ◆

Having your very own house is an extraordinary accomplishment. This is the reason people who don't have one imagined some time or another of purchasing their very own homes one day. At the point when that opportunity arrives, the fantasy is currently a reality, yet it is presently the journey with respect to where your fantasy home ought to be. Finding the correct spot for your home possesses become the following huge energy for you.

Since you have chosen to purchase a home, choose what amount it should cost. Expertise huge the house ought to be and in the event that you need a huge grass or not. Set it recorded as a hard copy how much your home should cost you. Be reasonable and don't overrate or under value your fantasy home. This is the place where "realizing what you truly need" is significant. It is your fantasy home. Thusly, it ought to be something other than what you need.

To be progressively exact, you should initially know where your home ought to be. You can pick the present city you live in as the spot for your home. It is completely up to you. Consider the area dependent on your inclination: do you appreciate city life or the calm nation? In the wake of comprehending what you truly need, you would now be able to begin searching for that ideal spot. This will rely upon the amount you can bear the cost of as costs of parts in the city could cost significantly more than parcels in the nation.

House and parcel bundles are the most prescribed alternative for would-be property holders. This spares you the time and bother from procuring modelers and contractual workers for structure and development. The drawback is that you have a home in where you needed to live, however you may wind up with a home that didn't coordinate what you envisioned it to be. Subdivisions are well known with house and part bundles, yet additionally consider real estate properties, which have extraordinary areas in urban communities that are available to be purchased. So, cautiously think about this before settling on an official conclusion.

Searching for the ideal area for your fantasy home could take some time, yet it will be justified, despite all the trouble. The land where your fantasy house will be is also part of your home, so set aside the effort to locate the ideal real estate parcel that where your own haven ought to be. Your spending limit likewise influences where that land ought to be. As we talked about before, lands in the city will cost more than grounds in the nation.

Obviously whoever is hoping to sell a house is doubtlessly going for the highest offer. Be that as it may, this isn't generally the most ideal approach, from the merchant's point of view. There are numerous, interesting points other than the cost when your hoping to sell your home.

You may be amazed by what you've recently viewed previously. It's very regular; we as a whole need to make the best out of any arrangement, particularly when selling our home. Anyway, this isn't generally the sharpest course for a merchant to take.

However, you have to contemplate some huge perspectives before setting up an extremely high selling cost. Enlisting a real estate professional can be an answer for a ton of situations you may have.

Sure going through some extra money on a real estate specialist doesn't sound excessively incredible. In any case, when you realize he will bring you nothing else than an extraordinary safe lawful arrangement, you ought to reexamine procuring a real estate professional. The vast majority are typically disheartened by the expense most real estate agents charge, yet most real estate professionals are constantly worth that little expense.

Above all else, setting an excessively significant expense can just push a ton of purchasers away. Then again, approaching a lower-than-should be expected cost for your home can't in any way, shape or form present to you any advantages. Perhaps the hardest part about selling real estate is deciding this perfect cost, so you draw in genuine purchasers without missing out on potential cash.

As you see, you have to build up some sort of harmony between the two wrong costs and concoct the correct one. A real estate agent can truly come in exceptionally helpful with regards to deciding the correct beginning selling cost for a house, in view of his experience into the field. The worth which they are giving you is much worth their expense. They will have the option to rapidly offer your home to a certified purchaser, without having you pass up a great many dollars.

He is definitely a natural to the house selling business sector costs in the region your house is in. You will need to set an aggressive cost for your home, since you wouldn't need any potential purchaser to turn their head and turn away subsequent to seeing your "available to be purchased" sign.

Realizing a normal selling cost for comparable properties in your general vicinity will sure guide you for making a sensible offer. Make a point to set up littler costs in the event that you plan on selling the house truly quick, and bad habit refrain.

When selling a property, probably the greatest thing you need to think about is setting the selling cost. Set it excessively high and you could frighten potential purchasers off. Set it excessively low and you end up not getting the best an incentive for your speculation. So how would you approach setting the correct sticker price for your property? One thing that could help you is a similar market examination or CMA.

A CMA is an archive that could differ from a two-page to a 50-page report. This would incorporate a few assumes that would enable you to choose the correct cost for your home. Fundamentally, a CMA contains your opposition as these are real estate properties that are in the market or has been there as of late.

When scrutinizing a CMA, you would see various information. In setting a cost for your home, there are sure gatherings that you should take a look at. First of all, the gathering of sold postings would give you an awesome thought how much houses are being sold for in the market as of late. This would give you a decent starting point in deciding the price that you would put on your property before you show it available to be purchased.

The subsequent stage for you to take is to discover comparative properties with the goal that you can get a decent correlation. For instance, deciding the present market as an incentive for your one-story house would be hard in the event that you just contrast it with a three-story property. That said, let us take a look at what you should search for in a property to contrast with your home.

One of the main things to search for is properties that have comparable area as your property. Appraisers generally put together their last figures with respect to this and it merits remembering that bigger square-foot homes are normally worth not exactly littler square foot houses.

Something else is the age of the house. Since models in development and the character of houses change with time, it is significant that you contrast your property and as of late, sold ones which are constructed an inside a couple of long periods of yours. This would give you a superior thought regarding the value that your home would order in the market.

There are three things that each home purchaser is searching for and these are area, area, and area. Consequently, you should contrast your property with as of late sold houses in a comparable area as yours.

When playing out a Comparative Market Analysis (CMA) to decide the asking cost before you sell your home or apartment suite, the typical path is to take a look at the latest practically identical deals. In any case, consider the possibility that there are no tantamount deals. Consider the possibility that a townhouse complex or neighborhood is generally little and there is almost no turnover of the properties. How would you gauge the present market estimation of a property you wish to sell when nothing around you has sold for a long time or more and costs have gone up or down fundamentally?

An inquiry came up over supper with certain companions an evening or two ago regarding how you would explain this evaluating difficulty. My companions have a townhouse in Complex GC, an inside unit that has been pleasantly refreshed. Since the last deal in their complex happened almost 2 years back, and costs have changed a considerable amount since 2005, this was going to take some work. One thought that struck us was to utilize the market information from other apartment suite deals in close by networks that are of comparable quality, so as to extrapolate an expected equitable incentive for their property.

The technique I used to guesstimate the present honest estimation of their property included doing broad unit by unit deal correlations for as far back as five years of the properties sold in 3 other close by condominium networks that I will allude to as TC, WM and MT. By assessing different units that were comparative in area, number of rooms, washrooms, area, and other applicable highlights, I had the option to adopt a chronicled strategy to deciding relative qualities for the properties that sold. Taking a look at 5 years of offers, I endeavored to scientifically extrapolate verifiable varieties in value per square foot and the connections between comparable quality units in every unpredictable.

The explanation behind returning 5 years was to guarantee that the information being utilized to extrapolate a present honest cost for Condo GC considered whatever number pertinent deals as could reasonably be expected over a significant stretch of time. This smoothed out any value abnormalities that may have happened with individual deals. Any one specific deal may be a deal or overrated in relative terms, dissecting 5 years of information limited those mutilations.

The authentic information demonstrates that condos in TC sell in a range that is between $80 per square foot to $100 per square foot more than comparative quality apartment suites in the GC complex. It is to some degree uncommon that this value differential can be extrapolated dependent on dollars per square foot instead of a differential dependent on a level of authentic deal costs. Ordinarily, one would expect that there would be a predictable rate differential as opposed to a hard dollar differential when contrasting units between the two edifices. There were insufficient deals in edifices MT or WM over the multi-year time frame to bring about any huge information that would influence the appraisals being made.

It gives the idea that the essential explanation that condos in TC sell at a greater expense for every square foot are because of the way that basically the majority of the units have carports, the properties are more current in development and the complex has broad courtesies including a pool, tennis courts, spa, clubhouse, practice room and other basic territory offices, when contrasted and the comforts for Condo GC. Different components that one must consider when playing out this kind of investigation incorporate the area of the unit in the complex and whether a property is an inside unit or an end unit. In the event that updates have been played out that would surely give, increased the value of any property and this can shift significantly all around.

The latest offers of updated units in TC have been from $492 per square foot up to $524 per square foot. This would demonstrate a present equitable incentive in

Complex GC, for comparable quality apartment suites, in the scope of $412 to $444 per square foot dependent on the verifiable value differential of $80 to $100 per square foot and how widely a unit has been overhauled. Excellent overhauls all through can have a colossal effect by the way you value a property available to be purchased.

One other significant factor to consider is that an inside unit will commonly sell for not exactly an end unit of similar quality. It's only an unavoidable truth that most apartment suite landowners in Incline Village and other retreat networks need an end unit and are happy to pay a premium for one.

For single family private deals, this procedure is a hell of much increasingly confused, particularly in a network like Incline Village at Lake Tahoe where there are no tract homes and for all intents and purposes each house is extraordinary. Get the job done is to state that you can't simply take a look at what the neighbor's place sold for.

Nobody can say without a doubt if this examination is the most ideal approach, as a ready purchaser and an eager dealer eventually decide the genuine equitable cost for any property. It does anyway give one approach to taking a look at evaluating how to value your property available to be purchased when there is no similar deals information to depend on. Regardless of whether a specific market is hot or cold, has a great deal of stock or is just months from the bustling selling season (as is commonplace of resort markets), there are numerous elements that will influence the ebb and flow market estimation of any property. In a real estate market, for example, Incline Village where there are for the most part custom homes and moderately couple of exchanges on a yearly premise, evaluating a property available to be purchased can be a confounded and interesting procedure.

One reason that I appreciate selling real estate in Incline Village and Crystal Bay is that it furnishes you with these sorts of difficulties all the time. Each home and apartment suite available to be purchased in Incline Village that I get the chance to see is novel here and there and until an arrangement closes escrow you never truly recognize what the honest estimation of a specific property genuinely is.

The strategies and date portrayed thus don't comprise a conventional examination or way to deal with doing property evaluations and ought not be understood accordingly. This article depicts one approach to attempt to gauge equitable worth dependent on a relative market examination utilizing information from the neighborhood MLS and the writer's involvement in an interesting retreat showcase. The creator is an authorized real estate operator, not an authorized real estate appraiser. The techniques portrayed above are for scholarly discussion just and not intended to substitute for an expert examination. The best way to get a precise gauge of the honest estimation of any property is to contract at least 1 authorized appraiser in your State and have a total evaluation performed of the subject property.

Despite the fact that getting as much benefit out of the clearance of your home seems like the objective, it isn't generally the best practice. Some of the time the best deals cost to put on your house isn't generally the most elevated.

This may appear to be unnatural to you. Obviously, we as a whole need to get however much cash-flow as could be expected when selling our home. Yet, first you have to choose what the objective of your deal is and how practical the cost is that you are inquiring.

Employing a real estate professional to help you in selling your home can be a keen move. A real estate agent can enable you to explore the way toward deciding your asking cost. The person can enable you to contemplate all viewpoints for setting your business cost.

It might appear to be pointless to pay a commission to the real estate operator from part of your benefit. In any case, that speculation can be little in the excellent plan of the selling procedure. Your real estate professional can guarantee you have a smooth and lawful selling procedure. Your real estate professional could likewise merit their bonus on the off chance that they help you locate the most noteworthy bidder and give you different tips on the best way to get that asking cost.

Deciding the cost at which to sell your home requires some work. Setting a business value that is excessively high in your market can ward off a potential purchaser. Then again, setting a too low deals cost on your home can draw in inappropriate purchasers or set you up to lose cash that you didn't have to lose.

A real estate professional can be your best device in setting the correct cost at which to list your home. Your real estate agent's involvement with selling, advertise investigation and working with purchasers can be priceless.

The most significant thought is the present lodging business sector costs in your general vicinity. Your real estate professional will be comfortable with the market and can enable you to decide the most focused cost at which to list your home.

It is likewise critical to think about how rapidly you have to sell your home. If you are in a rush to get out from under your present home loan, consider setting your business cost underneath market esteem. Something else, realizing the normal selling costs for comparable properties in your neighborhood is the most ideal approach to set your posting cost and sell your home in an auspicious way.

The initial introduction factor in real estate is a major ordeal creator. Commonly, the initial introduction is more powerful than a point by point investigation of the home. We've all known about 'affection from the outset site'. We know it's only a platitude, however underneath a great deal of alleged 'idioms' is a piece of truth. Individuals work from feelings a great deal of the time. Either intentionally or sub-deliberately, we get an impression about things that trigger either positive or negative sentiments inside us.

When you assume the job of dealer, you need to comprehend the significance of initial introductions. If the purchaser gets a terrible early introduction, your odds of selling are decreased by a major edge. There are a couple of spots where you can improve the initial introductions of your home, and it's a gainful exercise for you:

The first and most clear region is the day that the potential purchaser really visits the home to see it firsthand. When they drive up your road, they start to shape their initial introduction. Supposing that they purchase, they'll be driving up this equivalent road. They take a look at the house you're selling, yet at the homes around it. That is the reason neighbors are so critical to home estimation. Your home should rate among the best ones that exist in that area, except if your making do with a low price tag.

A few things you ought to do before the home visit is evacuate dead plants, rake leaves, cut grass and generally tidy up the home zone. The carport is probably the greatest purpose of early introduction. If they like maneuvering into your garage, it will establish an extraordinary pace for the remainder of the home. Simply put yourself from the purchaser's point of view and consider what you'd like to experience on the off chance that it was you.

One region that some don't consider appropriate based on the photos you take for publicizing your home. These photos should be top quality and expert. In the present web world, such an extensive amount the home shopping completes on the web. If your house is recorded there, it should be exhibited in the same class as it very well may be. Furthermore, you ought to have the option to give the searcher the same number of various looks as they can get, so they feel from their hunt that they genuinely comprehend what the home resembles.

When you attempt to make sense of the approaching cost for your home, don't be concerned about asking companions. What's more, don't be immediately affronted by amicable analysis. Simply accept it for what it's worth and realize that various individuals respond contrastingly to specific circumstances. What's more, this is the manner by which it will go with planned purchasers. So tune in with a receptive outlook, and check whether you can improve anything to change any negative criticism.

CHAPTER TEN
HOW TO FINANCE RENTALS

♦ ♦ ♦

The mystery in real estate business is to utilize other individuals' cash. This is the way most real estate big shots are made. Not at all like customary private real estate contracts, real estate financing offers a lot more extensive money related choices, including loaning or financing from different monetary foundations. Exchanges like these call for better than expected arrangement abilities.

It's not prudent to put your very own cash in a real estate concerning a couple of significant reasons. To begin with, you will in general give a large portion of your benefits away by not utilizing your investment. Second, real estate is an extremely dangerous business – you would prefer not to imperil all that you have.

It is not necessarily the case that real estate investment is about misfortunes. Despite what might be expected. If you realize how to make cash work for you, you may really gather a lot of cash as a byproduct of your investment.

Here's the secret:

On the off chance that you buy a $100,000 property that expands a norm of 7% for each year (in reality that number could be higher or lower), you would see a net benefit from leasing your property bringing about a roughly 15% return.

In case you're content with little return of investment, you may settle with your 15%return. Be that as it may, if you really need to acquire on your investment, think about what utilizing can accomplish for you. At present, a common real estate investor can discover financing as high as 95 to 97% of the price tag. There even a few occasions where you might probably get a 100 % financing yet we won't utilize this for our model as it's a deficient correlation.

Along these lines, in case you're an investor who is content with a small return of investment then 15% seems like a great deal. Be that as it may, for the individuals who really need to become wildly successful in the real estate, 15% is a long way from being viewed as a vital return.

How does utilizing work?

How about we expect that the rental pay will cover every one of your costs, including the home loan installments. Taking a similar model, a 7% valuation for your property brings about a $7,000 benefit for each year. With a 95% financing set up, you'll have the option to get a $7,000 return on $5,000 (your 5% initial installment on a $100,000 real estate property). This will furnish you with a 140%return on your investment. Not just that, with the equivalent $100,000 you can go out and buy 20 investment properties, money 95% % of them, and make an astonishing $140,000 benefit a year. This thoroughly beats the $15,000 benefit with an all-money exchange.

Regarding the extra 20 properties, hope to experience considerable difficulties getting financing for them since generally, just five or six new rental property home loans are the most extreme that banks by and by permit. Which is the reason you need a better than expected arrangement aptitudes.

Innovative Methods for Financing a Rental Property Purchase

The conventional way to purchasing an investment property is to set aside cash for an upfront installment. At that point, you should get a home loan to cover the rest. In any case, that is by all account not the only way. Every once in a while, I get inquiries from the landowners who asks questions about how they can back a rental property in the event that they need more in the bank for an upfront installment.

Here are the four techniques proposed for thought.

1. Dealer Financing

This includes getting an advance from the individual you're purchasing the property from. At times, if the merchant is eager to loan you cash, it's simpler (read: less desk work) than getting an advance from a bank.

I've seen these arrangements work in various situations: The merchant may back either the initial installment or the full price tag. The merchant may be another property investor — or they may be the property's live-in owner.

The way to progress is to guarantee you concur on a reasonable financing cost for the advance. In the event that you don't have much involvement here, it might be shrewd to work with your CPA or potentially lawyer. What's more, paying little heed to how much encounter you have, make certain to get the provisions of the credit recorded as a hard copy, with marks.

2. Organizations

Another extraordinary financing choice is to collaborate with somebody who has enough cash for an initial installment. This is a compelling system on the off chance that you have a companion or relative who's keen on engaging in property investment, however, perhaps isn't as interested by the everyday work of screening tenants and gathering rent installments.

In this situation, what frequently happens is that one accomplice sets up cash and different handles all the real work of being a landowner. I suggest considering it as far as adjusting the hazard and reward to expenses and advantages. Your accomplice is going out on a limb on all the budgetary risks; however you're placing in all the legwork of acquiring income by means of lease. Ensure the manner in which you split continues mirrors your commitments.

Whatever you choose bodes well, it's ideal to have your terms recorded as a hard copy.

3. Government Programs

The Federal Housing Administration (FHA) was established to support homeownership. One of the manners in which it does that is by offering homebuyers the opportunity to purchase property with only 3.5% down.

While FHA advances are explicitly intended to encourage the purchase of owner-involved homes, it's totally reasonable to purchase a two-, three- or four-unit building, live in one unit, and procure rental pay from the others. Truth be told, this can be an unbelievably savvy approach to back a rental property, particularly if it's your first.

FHA credit cutoff points are distinctive in each region, so part of the craftsmanship here is ensuring where you need to purchase is sufficiently high that you can buy a multiunit property.

4. Retirement Accounts

Many individuals who have changed occupations every now and again or worked for themselves for any time allotment have retirement cash in an IRA. If you have a self-coordinated IRA, you're permitted to put resources into nontraditional resources, which means an option that is other than stocks or shared assets. Real estate is an affirmed investment class, which means you can utilize cash in a self-guided IRA to back a rental property.

In the event that you go this course, however, chat with your CPA first. Indeed, even with programming that makes it simpler to be a landowner, real estate is a bigger number of hands-on investment than anything in the financial exchange. Before you dive in, prepare sure you're to contribute the time and vitality important to see an advantageous degree of profitability.

Keep in mind; Pay Attention to Details

Despite how you fund your rental property, make sure you have sufficient desk work set you up for progress and consistent pay from the property you purchase. That implies putting resources into:

- Formal agreements with a dealer who has consented to loan you cash toward a property buy.
- Legal records like an LLC working consent to characterize who does what in an organization (and who gets what remuneration).
- Projections are expected from different investment types from your monetary organizer so you can look at potential results.

Putting resources into real estate can be fulfilling and rewarding. To get the best advantage as long as possible, it's ideal to deal with the subtleties from the earliest starting point.

Financing Multiple Rental Properties

Purchasing various rental properties is, to be sure, a rewarding endeavor, particularly on the off chance that you are hoping to develop your real estate investment portfolio rapidly. Not exclusively would it be able to enable you to develop your investment portfolio, yet this methodology will also give numerous salary streams every month. Things being what they are, the reason doesn't each apprentice real estate investor do this? Since they do not understand how to back various rental properties without a moment's delay. Indeed, the general concept appears to be outlandish for generally amateurs.

Presently, in spite of the fact that it is difficult, we have assembled a couple of alternatives that will unquestionably enable you to figure out how to fund various rental properties. Along these lines, right away, here we go!

One Loan, Multiple Rental Units

One approach to back various rental properties is to purchase numerous units in a single structure. A wide range of multi-family real estate fall inside this classification including condo structures just as duplexes and quadruplexes.

All in all, how can one fund various rental properties of this type?

You can apply for standard home loan credits at the bank. The home loan you would get the chance to purchase a house to live in, with a couple of additional necessities, obviously. Be that as it may, you should fire setting something aside for an initial installment for investment property route before you look for subsidizing. Ordinarily, it is a 20% initial installment. Be that as it may, you can discover contract loan specialists who will require less.

Financing Two to Four Rental Properties

How to back numerous rental properties when you're thinking about purchasing less than 5?

You can go to your neighborhood home loan representative or bank for investment property financing. For this number of rental properties, you need the following:

1. A FICO assessment no under 630

2. An initial installment for investment property prepared

3. A quarter of a year of money holds for the ideal home loan installment

Be that as it may, one thing you have to remember is the sort of bank you go to. It's ideal to maintain a strategic distance from real banks. More often than not, such banks will in general be careful with the borrowers, so they require stricter criteria. Rather, work with nearby agents and search for banks which are typically more eager to fund under five rental properties.

Financing Five to Ten Rental Properties

For this number of rental properties, the bank will back your real estate investments if:

1. You have a FICO rating of 720

2. You have a half year worth of stores for assurance against opportunities

3. You have an upfront installment of 25% for single family homes and 30% for multi-family real estate properties

4. You don't have any history of dispossessions or chapter 11

5. You didn't fall behind on home loan installments for the most recent year

Financing More Than Ten Rental Properties

For this amount of real estate investment, you need to go to significant loan affiliations, for example, Bank of America. However, much the same as different choices, you should have your financial assessment prepared just as your upfront installment.

Is It Possible to Take Multiple Mortgages for Rental Properties?

Indeed, it is conceivable to take a few home loans to fund numerous rental properties. Nonetheless, the quantity of home loans will rely upon your home loan bank and its restrictions. Some will give you a chance to take the same number of as is allowed and others will restrict you dependent on your FICO assessment and capacity to cover installments. Along these lines, for this, you should perform appropriate due persistence.

Step by step instructions to persuade your home loan bank to back different rental properties for you

Most importantly, ensure you are prepared for the amount of desk work the loan specialist will be required. Your home loan bank ought to have the option to compute your obligation to-pay proportion which changes with each rental property investment you make.

Thus, set up the entirety of your budget reports just as other money related information that the loan specialist requires. You will require these to confirm your ability to reimburse the home loan.

Second, incorporate computations of the home loan in your marketable strategy. It must comprise of the measure of upfront installment you can give, the sum you anticipate that the bank should offer and the measure of regularly scheduled installment you can pay. You can utilize a home loan mini-computer for exact outcomes.

Prior to you even conversing with a bank about how to back various rental properties, feel free to make sense of certain numbers. Figure all the arrival on investment measurements, for example, the income, the top rate and the money on money return for every one of the rental properties. You need high rates to persuade them all things considered. Additionally, examine the area and discover about rates just as rental interest in that nearby showcase. At long last, set up everything together in a real estate marketable strategy and give it to your home loan banks.

How will you compute all that?

To play out a total and intensive rental property examination, you will require a number cruncher. It will likewise fill in as a home loan number cruncher by considering how all the home loan information you accommodate it influences the ROI of a rental property.

Step by step instructions to Finance Multiple Rental Properties: Other Ways

Despite the quantity of rental properties you are attempting to subsidize, different techniques may require somewhat more from you. For instance, you can go with a sweeping home loan however be prepared to confront its dangers.

You can also go to hard cash banks. Be that as it may, be prepared to reimburse the home loan in a brief period. Else, you may be liable to abandonment.

HOW TO REPAIR AND MAINTAIN PROPERTIES

Probably the greatest choice you will make as a landowner is whether you should enlist a property management organization or not. Numerous landowners oversee properties all alone or with the assistance of a representative, for example, an inhabitant administrator. Once in a while, it happens that landowners need more help when property issues are difficult. This is when landowners need to look for the assistance of real estate property management organizations.

Real estate property management organizations can be a colossal resource for your organization yet they don't come modest. They manage prospects and inhabitants, sparing you time and stress over advertising your rentals, gathering rent, dealing with support and fix issues, reacting to occupant objections, and notwithstanding seeking after expulsions. A decent property management organization brings its skill and experience to your property and gives you the significant serenity that accompanies realizing your investment is in great hands.

A real estate management business is a self-employed entity and this causes you to stay away from the issues of being a business. Along with the benefits, enlisting a real estate property management organization likewise accompanies a disadvantage of being a costly one. If you are living a long way from your rental property, it will be hard for you to deal with property issues from a far distance. The vast majority of the landowners anticipate discovering great tenants to keep up their property in great and appealing condition.

In actuality, there are not many landowners who look at their property as an investment and are not keen on loaning them to any occupants. For this situation, the best choice is to procure a real estate property management to deal with the property and deal with the related issues. Regardless of whether you appreciate hands-on management, you will come up short on time to focus on the development of your business which will place you in a circumstance to contract help for your property. Enlisting the help of a real estate property management organization is an appealing choice on the off chance that you can bear the cost of the expenses for the equivalent. While talking with management organizations, hope to hear statements running somewhere in the range of 5% and 10% of what you gather in lease income.

A rental property won't appreciate long-term occupant maintenance and satisfactory standard of profitability except if it is kept up appropriately. This includes:

- Preventive and continuous upkeep;
- Repairs to address issues or breakdowns;
- Construction and redesign

The Role and Responsibilities of a Rental Property Manager

Keeps up property rentals by promoting and filling openings; arranging and implementing leases; keeping up and verifying premises.

A property chief is an outsider who is contracted to deal with the day by day tasks of a real estate investment. They can deal with a wide range of properties, from single family homes to enormous high rises. Duties can be very expansive, including keeping up property rentals by filling opening, arranging and upholding leases, setting and collecting rent, screening forthcoming occupants, taking care of protests, keeping a precise spending plan and keeping up and verifying premises.

The property director is in the middle of the inhabitant and you, the owner. They are the "principal line of resistance" and they are there to secure you, to deal with all issues so effectively that furious tenants or specialist organizations are not calling you in the night.

In relation to physical upkeep and fixes, a portion of the particular duties may include:

- Investigating and settling inhabitant disagreements; reviewing empty units and finishing fixes; arranging remodels; contracting with explicit upkeep administrations, for example, carpentry, plumbing, power, finishing and snow evacuation administrations
- Supervising fixes.
- Establishing and implementing preparatory strategies and techniques; reacting to crisis.

Magnificent property chiefs are proactive and thorough.

Protection and Ongoing Maintenance

Preventive and progressive support of rental properties requires an exhaustive information of the property, its requirements for upkeep, staffing required to achieve the errands and planning to achieve them. The real estate property director must adjust the expenses of standard and preventive upkeep with the advantages and wanted outcomes. Details on a property supervisor's normal support rundown may include:

- Cleaning of normal regions;
- Landscape upkeep;
- Regular administration to warming and cooling frameworks;
- Periodic examination of pipes and electrical things;
- Proper upkeep of wood, material and other structure parts.

Fixes (Repairs) and Corrective Actions

Repairs and corrective activities are required when things break or stop to work as proposed. At times, the fix is of a crisis nature, for example, a warming breakdown in winter, while at different occasions these fixes can be booked and done productively in gatherings. It is the duty of the property director to know the distinction and to serve the requirements of the occupants while adjusting costs. It's additionally critical to deal with little issues before they become huge ones.

Development and Remodeling

Development and renovating are a piece of the office and building support. Redesign or development of the structure may be required:

- For exceptional business prerequisites of a business inhabitant;
- To right out of date quality of the structure; or
- To oblige uncommon physical needs of an inhabitant.

A real estate property supervisor can be extremely gifted at all different elements of management. However, if they fail with regards to office upkeep, the property will encounter a debasement of condition, loss of occupants, and declining rents.

Maintaining and Up-keeping a Real Estate Investment Property

We chat on and on about how you can possess a real estate investment property or how to put resources into real estate, yet what individuals frequently overlook is the significance of dealing with their real estate property. Like whatever else throughout everyday life, your real estate investment property needs uncommon and fastidious consideration to be fruitful and remain effective. So by what means can real estate investors keep up their real estate investment property? What is required to keep up predictable inhabitance in their rental properties? Give us a chance to discover.

Owning a real estate investment property can be exceptionally useful and can turn into a fundamental hotspot for your pay. It accommodates numerous individuals' extraordinary income, leaving them with additional cash, even after every one of the bills have been paid. The individuals who claim real estate investment properties have the benefit of controlling their prosperity or their disappointment. They get the chance to control the circumstance and their money related future. Some portion of expanding your prosperity and advantages from your real estate investment property is figuring out how to look after it. There are numerous preferences to keeping your property slick and clean. A well maintained property would maintain worth and draws in better quality inhabitants, which benefits the two sides.

Tips and rules on the best way to keep up real estate investment property:

1. Investigate both the outside and inside of your rental property

Having your rental property well-kept and free from any harms will build your benefit and enable you to clutch great inhabitants. Unanticipated costs like fixes and substitutions are unavoidable when dealing with a rental property and you shouldn't put them off. Here is a rundown of things to search for when examining your rental property.

Outdoor

Roof: verify whether there are missing shingles, harmed blazing or shape and greenery. These can cause expensive harms later on. Additionally verify whether there are any trees that expand onto your rooftop and cut them off. You need to abstain from having any of these since it very well may be a real side road for a large number.

Windows: verify whether every one of your windows are fixed appropriately without any holes and if there are holes, seal them. This will spare you later on from dampness harm and warmth lost.

Exterior painting: ensure that the outside of your rental property is constantly painted, so as to shield it from dampness and sun damage. No one needs to live in a house that looks terrible outwardly.

Landscape: check for broken tree limbs or trees with parasite. Anything that may be a problem to your occupants, make sure to fix it. Also ensure the grass is sound and consistently cut it with the goal that any new occupants going by could see that your property is well-kept up.

Indoor

Water radiator: make a point to deplete and consistently expel any soil from the water warmers. If you live in a territory with a great deal of silt in the water, you should seriously think about making this a month to month task.

Smoke indicators: this is certainly an absolute necessity. Continuously watch that your smoke alarms have new batteries. Living in a house with smoke alarms that don't work can be extremely hazardous.

Heating and cooling: you ought to consistently assess the warming and cooling framework. Check the channels and ensure there aren't any plants developing around them.

Paint: check for any paint chippings or shape that may be on the dividers and consistently re-paint your dividers for a spotless and crisp inside.

2. Keep your tenants happy

One of different ways you can keep up your real estate investment property isn't by fixing harms in your property, yet additionally keeping your occupants fulfilled. Only a basic examination to perceive how things are going or inquiring as to whether they need anything will work. Demonstrating to them that you are consistently there to help and that their fulfillment is your need will really have any kind of effect. This will help with your notoriety for future tenants and will draw in numerous individuals to your rental properties. React to their fix demands. One of the principle reasons tenants move out is on the grounds that they are upset, so make a point to keep your occupants satisfied.

3. Contract a property director

Dealing with your rental property can turn into a mind-boggling task. It requires some investment and necessities ordinary checkups. For the individuals who feel it's a lot of an over-burden, they can employ a property director that will keep up their real estate investment property. It is a major choice since these administrations are exorbitant yet consider all the time you will spare. A property supervisor can do all that you need from inside to outside to dealing with the month to month lease.

4. Adhere to the Landlord Occupant Law

Adhering to the landlord occupant law will help you in keeping up your real estate investment property and help you in overseeing it accurately. It will give a structure to both you and the inhabitant in order to not commit numerous errors and keep your rental property in great condition. One of the commitments under the landowner law is upkeep so adhering to this law accurately will profit you a great deal.

5. Revamp and Improve

Tenants are continually looking for new and created rentals. As an owner, you ought to consistently consider approaches to revamp and improve your real estate investment property. For models, including another style of outside plan, such as overhauling the yard or including a nursery, or modernizing the inside by including frameless glass dividers. Do some exploration on new inside structures that are moderate. These better than ever changes will draw in tenants from everywhere.

Tenants reserve the privilege to appreciate a protected and tenable living condition and it's the homeowner's obligation to deal with and keep up the property. A well-kept property will help increase your prosperity and income. Continuously discover approaches to settle rental property issues before the issues get greater.